To Jennifer
Enjoy the book!
Cheers,
Adele

About the ASAE-Wiley Series

All titles in the ASAE-Wiley Series are developed through a publishing alliance between ASAE: The Center for Association Leadership and John Wiley & Sons to better serve the content needs of member-serving organizations and the people who lead and manage them.

SPIKE YOUR BRAND ROI

How to Maximize Reputation and Results

ADELE CEHRS

Foreword by Sam Horn

Jossey-Bass books and products are available through most bookstores. To contact Jossey-Bass directly call our Customer Care Department within the U.S. at 800-956-7739, outside the U.S. at 317-572-3986, or fax 317-572-4002.

Wiley publishes in a variety of print and electronic formats and by print-on-demand. Some material included with standard print versions of this book may not be included in e-books or in print-on-demand. If this book refers to media such as a CD or DVD that is not included in the version you purchased, you may download this material at http://booksupport.wiley.com. For more information about Wiley products, visit www.wiley.com.

Library of Congress Cataloging-in-Publication Data

Library of Congress Cataloging-in-Publication Data has been applied for and is on file with the Library of Congress.
ISBN 978-1-118-97666-1 (hbk.); ISBN 978-1-118-97667-8 (ebk.); ISBN 978-1-118-97668-5 (ebk.)

Printed in the United States of America
FIRST EDITION
HB Printing 10 9 8 7 6 5 4 3 2 1

Contents

Foreword

Adele Cehrs attended a program I presented at ASAE's Annual Conference in Dallas, Texas, in which I introduced a method that shows how to create a one-of-a-kind competitive edge to make your priority project stand out in a crowded marketplace.

Adele was the star in one of our practice pitch sessions. I was impressed with her crackerjack smarts about the PR/marketing industry, and we continued our conversation following my program.

As soon as I heard about Adele's innovative approach for "Maximizing or Minimizing Your 15 Minutes of Fame or Shame," I told her, "That's a million-dollar idea. You've got to write a book about that."

Here it is!

Did you know *Advertising Age* reports there are 35 companies in the United States that spend more than $1 billion on advertising every year? The list includes such household names as Disney, Apple, Ford, Comcast, and #1 ranked Proctor and Gamble, which spends more than $10 billion globally every year.

Think about it. That's the advertising budget for just 35 companies. That doesn't include the advertising, marketing, and PR budgets for all the other companies in the United States and worldwide. We're talking about hundreds of billions of dollars spent trying to influence buyer behavior.

The problem? As Adele reveals in this book, all that money that companies, associations, government agencies, and nonprofits spend on PR and marketing can come crashing down with one poorly managed crisis.

Because understand this: if you're in business, something will go wrong. It's only a matter of time. And, something will go right. Are you prepared to mitigate the PR fallout and damage of a disaster or leverage the positive potential of a success?

Imagine if you were able to predict the SPIKEs of media attention—for better or for worse. Imagine being able to mobilize a preprepared crisis management plan for when it hits the fan. Imagine being able to capitalize on favorable media buzz when your business, product, or CEO are in the news for good reasons. Imagine being able to triage your marketing dollars so you spend them only when you are top of mind with your target customers.

You don't have to imagine it. That is what Adele's book *SPIKE Your Brand ROI* is about to teach you. You're about to discover why premier companies such as Yum Brands, Lockheed Martin, and DuPont have hired Adele to guide their strategic marketing. You're about to discover why her speaking engagements are packed with fans who love her humor, interactive exercises, and pragmatic recommendations that they can use instantly to reap real-world results and revenue.

In case you're wondering, "What's a SPIKE?" a SPIKE is a **S**udden **P**oint of **I**nterest that **K**ick-starts **E**xposure: It is a span of time when you and what you care about are thrust into the public eye. This can be cause for despair or cause for delight. By identifying your endgame and clarifying your goals and nonnegotiables, you can turn a SPIKE into a strategic platform that actually increases respect from your target audience—or you can sit back and get skewered.

If you care about your organization's reputation and profits, if you care about the continued respect of your employees, members, and customers, this book is a must-have. Read it and reap.

Sam Horn, Intrigue Expert,
author of *Tongue Fu!* and *POP!*

Preface

I've always considered timing and focus to be the platinum standard for any social media, PR, marketing, or advertising campaign. I had also always considered this to be automatic and as involuntary as breathing. But, when I started seeing tons of content that made no sense—people news-jacking stories that were completely wrong for their brand and the promise of engagement as a marketing silver bullet—I knew something had to change. When I embarked on this project, it struck me that too few people were actually successful at showing the value of their marketing efforts. On closer inspections, my suspicions were confirmed.

Social media experts and content marketers were recommending that brands create more content on more channels. PR firms and advertising agencies were fighting for dominance in the content marketing space—all while their clients saw little or no return on investment. The term *brand nurturing* became increasingly more popular, and little to no strategy regarding timing was considered. The public was drowning in content.

Moreover, news media were beginning to weigh in on brand crises like never before. How a brand responded or didn't respond became mainstream news. Additionally, media were reporting on how the public was reacting on social media related to brand incidents and opportunities.

Most people that I've met—I'm talking about top-tier CEOs and CMOs—who have created amazingly successful marketing campaigns were not throwing more content at the problem: they were actually creating fewer, more targeted messages that broke through the noise. They used the newfound interest in brand response in the media and the public to propagate more coverage, viral content, and marketing initiatives that were heralded as "genius." What was their secret? Turns out they were using SPIKEs in a way to capture a brand moment.

So, I was onto something. I've assembled the very finest practices in this book, along with a free online, continually updated appendix of resources, unlikely sources, and unlikely results—all from the standpoint of pursuing timing and focus—SPIKEs, that is, as though they were the lifeblood of marketing success. Which they are.

The problem is that many of you are not taking care of this most basic element of effective marketing. Fortunately, you've come to the right place for a methodology that will get your organization back on track. You might not like the rigor, but you'll thank me when you are creating stellar campaigns that win awards, praise, and industry recognition.

Acknowledgments

I want to personally thank all of the corporate and association partners who shared their insights and enriched this book with their experience and knowledge. I'd also like to sincerely thank my staff at Epic PR Group, especially Jenna Gregory-Sperry, for all of their contributions to this book. A special thank-you goes to Sam Horn, who gave me the courage to bring this book to life.

Also, thank you to Suzi Wirtz for her insightful and meticulous editing talent.

Thank you to everyone who contributed to make this a collective success.

To my husband and my daughter, Erik and Sienna Cehrs, to whom I am eternally grateful for their love and support.

And to my parents, Jack and Lorraine Gambardella, who inspired the dreamer in me.

About the Author

Adele Cehrs, the owner of Epic PR Group, has served as PR strategist, corporate counsel, and crisis-management advisor for clients such as Yum Brands, DirectTV, Dole, Johnson and Johnson, DuPont, Lockheed Martin, Verizon, Monster, Georgetown Cupcake, Sara Lee, and the Convention Industry Council. Prior to owning her own company, Adele was an executive at top PR firms in New York City and Washington, DC, including TSI Communications and Ogilvy Public Relations Worldwide, and served as a spokesperson for companies such as DuPont, 1-800-Flowers, Transwestern Properties, MCI/WorldCom, and DirectTV.

She is a frequent media expert for CNN Headline News, NPR, Fox Business, CBS, NBC, Voice of America, *Inc., Bloomberg Businessweek, PRWeek, Forbes,* the *Wall Street Journal,* and *Entrepreneur* and has media-trained numerous CEOs, including Ted Leonsis, Marilyn Hewson (CEO of Lockheed Martin), and Steve Case. Adele also secured a reality show for Georgetown Cupcake called *DC Cupcakes* that airs on TLC.

Adele has spoken at hundreds of conferences including ASAE, Convention Industry Council, Inc. 500, IABC, PRSA, Digital Now, EO, the Global Social Media Conference in Boston, Las Vegas, and Dallas, and the Canadian Board of Trade. She was a top-rated speaker at ASAE's Marketing, Membership, and Communications Conference in 2011, 2012, and 2013.

Perhaps most important, Adele is considered a thought leader in her industry because she has catapulted virtually unknown businesses into becoming multimillion-dollar household names, including 1-800-Flowers.com and Georgetown Cupcake. She has codified her disruptive process into a step-by-step, replicable methodology called SPIKE that has received rave reviews from audiences and dramatic results for clients.

SPIKE YOUR BRAND ROI

What's Real Brand Engagement?

"A brand for a company is like a reputation for a person. You earn reputation by trying to do hard things well."
—JEFF BEZOS, founder of Amazon and owner of the *Washington Post*

Imagine this.

You're going about your day, scanning through the online news site, your feeds on Facebook, Twitter, Instagram, and LinkedIn. Some things you like, some things you share, you might comment here and there, some things you just scroll past, others you click through. This is what we call engagement. And this is great for brands. Right?

But fast-forward ten minutes. Twenty minutes. An hour. Maybe you remember one or two bits of content you saw today, but only because you're thinking about it.

Come dinner time, you've completely forgotten that you really loved the Papa John's heart-shaped pizza post on Facebook today, because you feel like tacos for dinner and barely remember you even saw it. **Do you really have any idea which brands *engaged* you today?**

It's estimated that people see five thousand brand messages a day, according to CMO.com. How do you break through the noise? How do you create real perception and behavior change? The first step is to remove the clutter and **focus on what really matters.**

Did You Know?

- In the United States alone it's estimated that businesses spend **$155 billion annually on advertising and PR** to get a brand into the public eye (Galant 2012).
- Research shows that marketers are getting worse, not better, at directing their dollars, with **a whopping 40 percent of marketing dollars being wasted each year** (Neff 2012).
- That means **$62 billion is misused** on content that is not relevant or producing ROI.

Tens of billions in wasted marketing every year. It's not smart. It's not strategic. Yet as evidenced by these alarming statistics, that's what many companies are doing. What if there were a better way? What if you could focus your energy and resources and money only when you are truly top of mind? What if you could have a higher spend-to-impact ratio? That is what *SPIKE Your Brand ROI* will teach you.

If you know how to prepare for, spot, and capitalize on a SPIKE—a <u>S</u>udden <u>P</u>oint of <u>I</u>nterest that <u>K</u>ick-starts <u>E</u>xposure— you will learn how to:

- Mitigate the damage or maximize the benefits by anticipating when you or your company, association, or nonprofit is going to be of interest
- Decrease your marketing spend while increasing your bottom-line benefits
- Prevent a public perception of catastrophe that damages the goodwill you spent years creating

Some experts tell you that it's vital for your organization to drop everything you are doing to respond to every comment or issue within your bailiwick. The truth is that your executives want—and need—some level of planning, ideation, and strategy before they commit to a position. The way to do that is to understand when your audience has the highest point of interest, a SPIKE. While it may sound impossible to make predictions about a brand's relevance, the truth is that brands have discernible patterns. Those patterns are driven by audience interests and outside events that require some real-time nimbleness.

The Consumer Electronics Association experiences a positive SPIKE every year with its world-renowned International Consumer Electronics Show—a technology smorgasbord of the goodies early adopters will be drooling over next year. More than 150,000 people flock to it from a variety of industries to see what's next or what's garnering buzz in consumer electronics.

General Motors experiences a negative SPIKE when it recalls millions of cars.

But what if you had more control, more ability to influence these SPIKEs?

You can.

People are interested in hearing from a brand when that brand has something to say that pertains to their lives—everything else you do in between is just a buildup or build down to major brand opportunities or crises. You might be thinking, "I'm not Consumer Electronics Association or General Motors, so how can I relate to such big-brand examples?" The process is the same for any entity handling issues or opportunities. You can learn from some of the big guys' mistakes.

We're flipping the traditional business communication model on its head. For decades, companies have been able to dictate when they are relevant to mainstream media. Now the audience dictates when they will care. It isn't just engagement for engagement's sake. It is about timing and knowing when your audience wants to hear from you.

What Exactly Is a SPIKE?

William Jennings Bryan once said, "Destiny is not a matter of chance, it is a matter of choice; it is not a thing to be waited for, it is a thing to be achieved." That is SPIKE—not something to wait around for, but something that you, your organization, and your marketing/PR team can achieve with the right tools and knowledge.

A SPIKE is a *Sudden Point of Interest that Kick-starts Exposure*. It is the opportunity to make or break you and your organization. It is a point in time when your industry, profession, or members are thrust into the public eye ... for better or for worse.

S – Stands for Sudden

>Communication that suddenly pops up doesn't qualify as a SPIKE unless it clearly meets two criteria: the opportunity that arises is central to your brand's message and the communication can be relayed to your audience within a finite, specific period of time.

P – Stands for Point

>There is a point, a single shining point in time, when you have the opportunity to change the conversation. To capitalize on the SPIKE you have to be nimble. You must react quickly and effectively to get the optimum benefit from sudden attention, a time when all eyes are on you, your company, or your cause. If you are quick and you have the right message, you can provide a solution, reaction, or point of view that is uniquely yours. If you're really good, you can even come to own a topic, and that can be a gold mine for months or years.

I – Stands for Interest

>The word *interest*, as a verb, means to excite curiosity or attention. Your audience, not your executive staff or board, must be interested in the topic. Too many times, organizations forget that in this decade, the audience is in control of when they will tune you out or sing your praises.

K – Stands for Kick-starts

>To kick-start something is to cause it to catch on or take off. In a SPIKE, you can kick-start attention by being the first and best to respond in real time to an evolving issue in the media, your industry, or your profession.

E – Stands for Exposure

>Exposure can be a positive or negative in marketing. If you don't control a SPIKE, if you do not have a plan of attack and excellent operational timing, you can leave your organization exposed to a negative SPIKE and create significant vulnerabilities. However, if applied correctly, you can anticipate those vulnerabilities and perhaps even benefit from them with strategic positioning and perfectly timed messages.

Relevance and Timing

Here's the bad news. Any company, cause, or creation, regardless of scope or scale, is only truly relevant to its audience a few times a year. That's it.

I am not talking about basic marketing and PR; that's what we marketers are paid to do at the most elementary level. I am not even talking about the marketing opportunities through the year with small to medium impact; those aren't SPIKEs.

I am talking about the moments when what you say and what you do has a major impact on your customers' business, behavior, and market—those select moments that transform campaigns, initiatives, and ideas into a remarkable shift in perception. That doesn't happen every day, and it shouldn't.

A SPIKE isn't like accounting or other orderly business functions that follow a specific pattern year in and year out. SPIKEs don't happen on a neat timetable such as quarterly, seasonally, or when your marketing team has time. They happen based on seemingly spontaneous market or media demands.

Now, I know you don't want a mediocre organization, or you'd have put this book down several pages ago. You don't want average results. You know you can't just keep doing what you are doing. But there's more to riding a SPIKE than that. It's a terrifying experience.

If you follow the advice I'm presenting in this book, it can go so right that you create game-changing wins that will elevate your career. It's not completely predictable, but if you seek epic results, read on.

2

Why Your Brand Doesn't Stand Out

"The only limit to your impact is your imagination and commitment."
—TONY ROBBINS

For those of you who are thinking, "But experts say we need to engage with people all the time because we need to create value all the time," my answer is, "No, you don't!" It is a form of brand narcissism to think people want to be engaged or communicated with *all* the time. People have too much content coming at them to tell when your messages really matter. And you are so busy communicating value that you miss big opportunities to challenge, exceed executive expectations, and create results that change behaviors and shift perceptions.

A recent Gallup Mobile Retail Panel Study conducted in January 2013 asked, "How much does social media impact your purchasing decisions?" Results showed that only 5 percent of people said that "social media had a great deal of influence over their purchasing decision." And, 63 percent said social had "no influence at all" (Swift 2014) (see figure 2.1).

In another yearlong study from the New Brunswick, NJ–based research firm the Keller Fay Group, 91 percent of respondents said they get information about brands as a result of face-to-face conversations or over the phone (Belicove 2011).

Moreover, a study published in the *Journal of Consumer Psychology* in 2014, titled "Why Recommend a Brand Face-to-Face but Not on Facebook," looked at differences between word-of-mouth

Figure 2.1.   Social Media Influence Based on Gallup Mobile Retail Panel Study.   *Source:* Courtesy of Epic PR Group

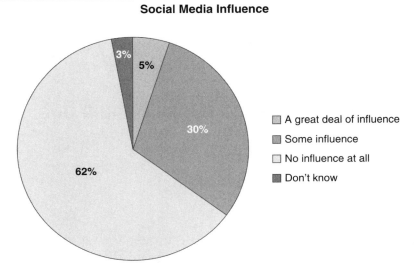

Social Media Influence

recommendations in social media and in person. Bottom line is people are far less likely to recommend brands to each other in social media channels because of what the study calls the perceived "'social risk' that social media recommendations entail ('social risk' [that] is the perceived risk to your public image and reputation if your recommendation doesn't pan out)" (Eisingerich, Chun, Liu, He, and Bell, 2014).

Turns out people don't recommend (often) on Facebook because Facebook recommendations are public, written, and broadcast (in contrast to the private, oral, and personalized one-to-one recommendations of traditional word of mouth).

These three studies beg the question: if people are engaging with your brand via social networking, does it equate to real behavior change, influence, or ROI? Not necessarily.

Remove the content clutter and focus on what really matters and you can stand out and create real ROI for your brand. Doing this doesn't have to lessen your budget's or your organization's effectiveness. It can actually increase ROI, respect, and results.

I'm not saying that social media or content marketing is ineffective; I am simply stating that your audience is seeing too much content to put any real value or sense of importance on your message, timing, or brand priorities to move them into action. That is why marketers need to change their strategy and create quality over quantity. This is where SPIKEs come in.

How Do Marketers Take Advantage of SPIKEs?

What does understanding SPIKEs mean for marketers? It means that you have finite moments in your career that can serve or sabotage your success, and it is up to you to get a seat at the executive table, acquire the resources you need to be successful, and demonstrate ROI. For CMOs, the stakes are even higher. A study from CMO.com showed that the average tenure of a CMO is 45 months, or four years, roughly half that of an average CEO's tenure (Douglas 2014). This gives each CMO and his or her staff a few critical chances to make a significant impact, or risk being replaced.

Why do you suppose there is such a massive divide between CMOs and CEOs? Statistics from Chief Executive.net state that, overall, "80% of CEOs claim they have lost trust in their marketers, and this has resulted in Chief Marketing Officers (CMOs) losing a seat at the strategic table, often ranking lower in title and stature and having a reduced scope of responsibility." The website also states that "because of the lack of trust in their marketers, CEOs have stopped imposing Key Performance Objectives (KPOs) and Key Performance Indicators (KPIs) for marketers" (Whitler 2013).

Additionally, I believe that CMOs and their communications and marketing teams are too busy proving the value of their work through metrics that are outdated or inaccurate to satisfy executives who demand accountability for campaigns they've asked for based on a "hunch." These initiatives are such a time suck that it leaves marketers unable to actually do the important work that matters. I've heard some of the best CMOs in the world complain about this problem. It is a constant balancing act to get the good ideas to rise to the top, while managing the expectations of executives who think they know how to do marketing.

How many times have you been called into a meeting with the CFO to brainstorm how he manages the company's finances? And how many brainstorming meetings have you been in with the COO to discuss operations and how to improve them? That's right, quarter past never. Yet, whenever a CMO or a marketer comes up with a new concept or initiative, we need to gain buy-in from executives who have little to no experience in our field but consider marketing "fun."

The only way we can change the way people view marketing and communications is to truly prove the value of our ideas and expertise by selecting only campaigns and ideas that will lead to real behavior change. That's what you can learn from using this unique marketing method called SPIKE.

Why Is It So Critical to Use SPIKEs?

With technology and social media as pervasive as they are today, studies show that our attention span is only eight seconds long (Greengard 2013). Consumers are bombarded by brand after brand on multiple channels in multiple forms. Our executive leaders in the C-suite are also on the same distraction cycle as the rest of us. They are looking for quick, easy solutions, not complex ideas that require strategy, timing considerations, and messaging. They want a quick fix, so they deploy what seems like the best use of resources—free social media. Except social media isn't free. It comes with a great cost, far greater than time. It is the cost of always being available for your audience. Always engaging, conversing, liking, tweeting, and sharing. What happens when something is too available? You abuse the goodwill of your brand loyalists by posting or retweeting irrelevant stories that have no bearing on your audience's decision making. Consumers and buyers can't retain or hold onto more-impactful interaction than that, pure and simple.

Simon Cowell, oftentimes blunt and even controversial, once said, "I hate clutter. It really bothers me because I can't think properly. If you've got distractions in front of you, your mind goes nuts" (Hardy 2009). My hope is that you'll find this book to be full of practical ideas that can fast-forward the success of your ideas and help you establish a new approach to marketing and communications by focusing on less, not more. So, can I be blunt? Remove the clutter from your current marketing or PR plan and focus on what really matters.

The good news is you can scale your results, reputation, and ROI by focusing on your SPIKEs.

The Best Way to Use This Book

As you read this book, identify four key issues that you or your organization are concerned or excited about. Although it might be hard to narrow down what's truly important, with some prioritization, it can be a freeing and exhilarating exercise.

- What do you want people to care about?
- What do you want people to repeat about your organization?
- What is a product or service you want the media and industry influencers to notice?
- What do you want people to buy from you?

The following chapters introduce specific SPIKE techniques and share compelling examples that demonstrate how the techniques work in a variety of situations. I also offer step-by-step approaches, valuable worksheets and assessments, and actual how-to exercises that you can apply to produce epic results. You will read examples of CMOs, marketing staff, and PR professionals who took a chance on a SPIKE and were hailed as "an unlikely PR genius," "the boldest campaign seen in decades," and "the marketer who could teach all marketers a thing or two."

By turning your organization's SPIKE into a strategic platform, you can obtain real ROI, or you can sit back and get skewered. Read on to learn how to

- Predict and minimize negative SPIKEs.
- Identify and track brand relevance.
- Create opportunity SPIKEs.
- Leverage positive (and negative) attention.

If you care about your organization's reputation, revenue, public perception, bottom-line profits, and employee and member satisfaction, this book is your must-have go-to guide. Get ready. You're about to read fun and fascinating success stories from a wide variety of people who have used the SPIKE technique to come up with innovative campaigns and pitches that helped them respond to a crisis, get noticed, and stand out in a sea of sameness. Turn the page and let's get started.

Brand Narcissism

"It's always about timing. If it's too soon, no one understands. If it's too late, everyone's forgotten."
—ANNA WINTOUR

The fashion industry considers timing the most important element in its decision to release a new line, update an old style, or discontinue an item. The fashion industry doesn't wait for trends; if their style doesn't match the runways, they create their own and make it seem purposeful. The fashion industry gets us to make purchases more often because of the seasonal nature of clothes and styles. This industry hangs its hat (pardon the pun) on the *when*.

Many other industries, however, ignore timing. Or, they become selfish—even narcissistic—making timing fit their need or announcement. They simply make it the last thing under consideration, especially when it comes to marketing. See if this case in point sounds familiar. If you've ever been in a meeting for a product launch or new concept, you can predict how the conversation will go. First, the person who thought of the idea will provide an overview. Next the room of executives will dissect the product or concept, consider its tactical and strategic merits, inquire about what the competition is doing in the same space, and decide whether to implement the idea or not. Finally, the executives will provide the idea to internal or external marketers, who will consider what channel is best for the announcement, create the announcement, and disseminate it with almost little or no thought given to the timing of that announcement. Timing is often an afterthought. Why is this so when it is the most important part of marketing?

Timing is what can make or break a SPIKE. Just like surfing, knowing how to spot the SPIKE, position yourself to catch it, and then ride it out is an art form and makes all the difference in where you end up.

From Aesop to Oprah

In Aesop's "Boy Who Cried Wolf" fable, a shepherd boy was tending his flock when he cried, "Wolf, wolf!" The nearby villagers ran up the hill to his aid, except there was no wolf. The boy was lying. Once again, a few minutes later, he cried, "Wolf, wolf!" And, once again, the villagers came running. Again, no wolf, and the boy took noticeable pleasure in watching the people walk away frustrated. Some length of time went by, and to the boy's dismay he found himself and his flock under the attack of a wolf. Panicked and in real need of saving, the boy called for help from the villagers. "Wolf, wolf!" he cried, but the villagers had become tired of his false alarms and didn't answer his call.

The same could be said for brands that are constantly shouting their own noise. They have an important product announcement. They have an anniversary. They are looking for feedback on a new conference, idea, logo, and so on. Or they post pictures of cats, dogs, and babies—which have little or no impact for their audience—to increase the EdgeRank Score. In fact, it is a blatant waste of their audience's time and attention. When a brand has a real story or value to share, their audience has become so tired of hearing from them that they miss out communicating the most important message. There is only so much your audience will put up with, just like the villagers in Aesop's classic tale.

How often is too often to share with your audience? Many companies, associations, and nonprofits are looking for the perfect amount of engagement. There are all kinds of prescriptions for frequency. According to an article in *Fast Company* published on April 15, 2014, companies should post to Twitter at least 5 to 20 times a day (600 per month). Social media experts recommend posting to Facebook 5 to 10 times per week (40 times per month).

And they suggest posting to LinkedIn once per day (20 times per month). That is an insane amount of content for the creator and the reader (Lee 2014).

Contrary to what other people say, I would contend that with every seemingly useless post, your audience becomes less engaged, not more. I've heard experts say, "It's about creating a best girl-friend relationship with the brand." But why would a brand like Walmart, Skittles, or Liberty Mutual Bank need to be my friend? I only want to hear from a company when it is important to me, not when it is important to the brand. It's about organizations balancing the "we" versus "me" mentality. The "we" is your audience and they decide what's important. The new reality is that organizations who understand this will come out on top.

Consider the Oprah Effect. In her heyday, being on *Oprah* affected companies, authors, and brands in a similar way. People and companies who were lucky enough to have a seat on her couch or were featured in her Favorite Things List or The Oprah Book Club would see "up to 1,000 percent growth over the short term immediately following the episode and sustained higher revenues for months or years afterward," according to Inc.com. "Many of these companies promote 'As seen on Oprah' on their sites and other marketing materials to help sustain that growth. And success breeds success: once you've been on *Oprah*, every other media outlet will give you a closer look" (Hornbuckle 2009). So what is the equivalent to Oprah in today's media world? That is what's so interesting.

We, as the consumers, members, and audience at large, are our own Oprah. We decide our "favorite things," and we decide how much we "talk" about a brand.

Regardless of the likes, tweets, and shares a brand receives in a day, many people couldn't tell you what content marketing relates back directly to the brand doing the promotion. As I stated earlier, we see 5,000 marketing messages any given day, far too many to be discerning. So how do we decide the brands that actually warrant our attention and time? We focus on brands that are judicious, that understand our desires and needs, and that deliver products, services, and information that relate to those needs at the time we need them—just like Oprah.

Oprah's programming was also selective. Yes, we joined her each and every day in our living room at 4:00 p.m. EDT for her shows, but she had a formula for what was worthy of her attention. The factors and formula were almost always the same. "Having a woman-owned business, being on the cusp of a new trend [which you can make up—see how at the end of this chapter], and serving a good cause. In short, having a compelling story that would speak to *Oprah*'s demographic" (Hornbuckle 2009). As someone who pitched and secured brands on Oprah's show, I could instantly tell which clients would realize the dream of being on *Oprah* and those who were delusional.

When you think of an idea for your business, who acts as your brand's internal or external Oprah? Who, if anyone, is discerning whether the message will truly appeal to your demographic? What is your formula for what is worthy of your audience's attention? Who is your Chief Oprah Officer?

If You Care, Don't Miss Out

Unfortunately, most marketing, PR, and social campaigns are run in such an insular manner that they don't reflect the company's or association's values. For instance, Urban Outfitters is facing a public backlash for selling a "Vintage Kent State Sweatshirt" that is spattered with red stains resembling blood. The $129 sweatshirt is reminiscent of the Kent State massacre of May 1970, when four unarmed college students were killed by the Ohio National Guard during a Vietnam War protest. In my opinion this type of negative attention was done purposefully to stay in the public's consciousness even if for negative reasons. Although these upticks in attention may work temporarily to increase traffic or conversation about the brand, I believe this type of opportunistic move will only hurt the brand in the long run. This is the type of SPIKE that comes back to haunt a brand and I don't recommend it. If the brand ever runs into trouble the public will remember these transgressions and be less likely to rally for the brand. No retail clothing brand should want to be associated with such a senseless act of violence, which has nothing to do with their goals as a company. They should instead focus on critical, related initiatives that match the company's brand goals.

I believe the reason this happens is that organizations put extremely young, inexperienced people in what I would argue is one of the most important jobs—analyzing and listening for trends online that pertain to offline business strategies. The person or team deciding what is important is too inexperienced in the world of perception, business, and leadership to make those critically important calls in brand perception. Let's take CVS as a case in point of one organization that gets brand listening right.

CVS Caremark brilliantly executed a PR campaign that would change the pharmaceutical industry forever. In early 2014, the retailer announced it was to stop selling tobacco products at 550 locations starting October 1, 2014. The company estimated that it would lose $2 billion in sales from customers buying cigarettes and other products. To put that in perspective, that is a fraction of its overall sales of $123 billion in 2012.

When you have a SPIKE, for better or worse, the busy world has stopped in its tracks to focus on your brand, organization, or industry. A SPIKE can sharpen your image, or stab you in the back. The move by CVS was hailed as "bold" by industry analysts and media personalities. CVS understood the essence of timing and how its positioning strategy would not only positively affect the brand but garner widespread support and put the company ahead of its competitors. They made a huge public health statement and didn't back down. But it didn't come out of thin air.

All the signs were there for those analyzing the CVS industry landscape:

- According to the *New York Times*, just 18 percent of American adults smoke, down from 42 percent in 1965 (Strom 2014). Clearly, CVS was changing its product strategy at a time when smoking was in decline.
- An op-ed published in the *New York Times* by two doctors from the Smoking Cessation Leadership Center at the University of California made the case for eliminating tobacco products from drugstores in the *Journal of the American Medical Association* published online.
- The FDA announced the start of a national education program aimed at preventing smoking among youth.

- CVS offers many healthcare-related services. On the heels of the company launching its own anti-smoking campaign, CVS could use this national platform to promote its healthcare-related offerings, which would appeal to a more sophisticated target market.

Clearly the company's executives must have understood the positive effects this strategy would have from a consumer perspective. And their swift and decisive action paid off, as President Obama even commended the company publicly and recommended other pharmacy chains to follow suit. An inexperienced brand perception team wouldn't have had the boldness to carry this off. And although not selling tobacco products may hurt CVS's profit margins for a while, this brand strategy will create billions in goodwill with more health-conscious consumers who will now proselytize CVS. The strategy was so strong that shareholders didn't flinch at the short-term profit margins; they knew they would be cashing in in the long run. CVS's recent PR move proves that with the right message, strategy, and timing, you can turn a SPIKE in attention into a platform, or you can sit back and get skewered, like RiteAid, Duane Reade, and Walgreens.

As you read the CVS example, you may be thinking, "CVS is a multimillion dollar company, and the pharmaceutical industry is one of the largest industries in America. How could this type of competitive analysis work for my company or cause? We're not nearly in the same arena." The good news is the signs are there regardless of the size of your organization.

How do you find out what the most important things are for your fans, members, and customers? Find the most polarizing people in your industry or profession. Think about why they elicit such strong opinions. Polarizers are those people in your industry or profession who can divide a room. What they talk about is often what a member or customer is truly concerned with. They reveal extreme views and fears. Often these people get dismissed as troublemakers, naysayers, and heretics. As Seth Godin wrote in the book *Tribes*: "heretics, troublemakers and change agents aren't merely thorns in our side, they are the keys to our success" (2008, 11). His book explains how to get the tribe motivated to talk, listen, and share ideas and when the best time is to do so.

You can have the biggest tribe in the world, but if you don't motivate them to act when you need them, then what's the point?

It's not about managing the tribe; it's about managing and *anticipating the reaction* to the message before it spreads in traditional media, on social media, in meetings rooms, or at your annual conference and tradeshow. You may not be able to control everything, but at least you can anticipate the vitriol. If you can get out in front of what others will say and predict it with a level of transparency, they will respect you. Take what happened to the Live Strong Foundation after Lance Armstrong, a hero to most Americans, was found out to be lying about doping allegations after winning the Tour de France seven times.

In a statement after Lance Armstrong appeared on *Oprah* and admitted his untruth, the Live Strong Foundation said, "Our success has never been based on one person—it's based on the patients and survivors we serve every day, who approach a cancer diagnosis with hope, courage and perseverance. We listened to their needs and took action to create free cancer support services that offer access to clinical trials, fertility preservation, insurance coverage and even transportation to treatment. People living with and through cancer are the inspiration behind our work. They have been, are and always will be our focus" (ET Online Staff 2013). The foundation's swift and strong message positioned them away from Lance Armstrong's controversy and rededicated them to their mission of serving and providing for cancer patients.

If you can anticipate what people will say and get ahead of their concerns in statements or new product announcements, you can save your organization a lot of time worrying about the polarizing.

Anticipate When Your Brand Loyalists Need to Hear from You

- Begin with one specific announcement or project in mind when doing this exercise.
- Identify the best times to market to an audience according to when they will make purchasing decisions or seek information about your organization. Realistically, customers have only

three to five times a year when they come to your organization for information, education, or to make a purchase. This is when you have the opportunity to sway them, change a perception, or get them to believe in your organization. All your marketing and communications campaigns and initiatives should begin with that in mind.

- Segment timing to specific personas of customer and member groups as well as individuals. Start with one group at a time.
- Do your best to guess which times they think about your organization, and then do more comprehensive research with focus groups, surveys, and in-person meetings.
- Talk to your prospects and customers to drive dialogues that lead to brand engagement and transactions.
- Build both quantitative and qualitative research questions with response alternatives to gain insights from customers. Conduct research and implement a process that identifies your firm's most powerful client consumption moments for marketing messages. Bring in the IT department to conduct basic analytics and see when people frequent your website most.
- Track and identify what is working in real time. At the end of 6 months, 9 months, and 12 months you can see which communications are trending and which ones are failing.
- Create a communications and marketing kill list to weed down needless communications. This will help you focus on when you are truly timing your communications correctly and when you are just crying wolf.

SPIKEs are ever present and must be anticipated and managed by every type of business, big or small. Experienced communications people look out for, and recognize, these brand opportunity patterns. The trouble is that their recommendations for a nimble response to burgeoning issues often fall on deaf ears with overly cautious executives.

SPIKE Assessment

"There is only one thing in the world worse than being talked about, and that is not being talked about."
—OSCAR WILDE

Do you know *when* your audience thinks your message is relevant to them? How is your marketing strategy working to predict when you are top of mind and to influence and better engage your audience?

Once you know what makes your content more interesting and valuable, it's time to positively position your organization for success and begin to greatly improve your impact ratio. It all begins with understanding timing and focusing on when your audience want to hear from you.

The SPIKE Assessment gives you the step-by-step method to understand how to look for and respond to a SPIKE. This short questionnaire will help you overcome your weaknesses, build your team, or capitalize on your wins. This book includes a private code to unlock one free online SPIKE Method Assessment. Based on some of my extensive interviews and research on the importance of timing, your customized online report will reveal *when* you can best influence others.

Unlike the online version, the SPIKE Self-Assessment in this chapter is a self-scoring quiz. Once you take it and see your score, use the following legend. If you score

- Between 0 and 35, don't put this book down; it's your new best friend.

- Between 36 to 70, good for you. You've had some practice at anticipating and leveraging your SPIKEs and you will be at the top of your game after reading this book.
- Over 70 to 100, congratulations! You obviously understand the importance of SPIKEs. The good news is you're going to find fresh examples and even more specific techniques in this book, which will help you get even better at it.

Self-Assessment

To make the most of the quiz, think of one project, product, or service that you want to get attention for or create an opportunity around. For example, if an organization like ASAE were to try and do this assessment for the association at large, that would be difficult. Therefore, I would encourage Mariah Burton-Nelson, ASAE's vice president of innovation and planning, to assess for the innovation department. Anne Boulin, director of education, would do the assessment for an upcoming keynote at a conference. Reggie Henry, chief technology officer, should assess for the website. And Robb Lee, chief marketing officer, should do it for member communications. I might even suggest John Graham, ASAE's CEO, take it to provide perspective on what ASAE should focus on as a whole. Here's the only caveat: collectively, you still come up with *only* three to five SPIKEs in an organization per year. That's it.

Once the assessment is complete, convene a strategy meeting and have everyone report back to each other to better understand how their SPIKE could take precedence or *not*. This will help crush silos and build consensus for what your organization should focus on.

1. Do you have a measureable goal for this year or every year?
   a. Yes
   b. No
2. Have you identified three SPIKEs this year that you plan to leverage when you are going to be top of mind for your audience?
   a. Yes
   b. No

3. Have you ever stopped an announcement, launch, or initiative due to poor timing or the feeling that you weren't addressing an issue at the right place or right time?
   a. Yes
   b. No
4. When is a time you were deliberately contrarian, controversial, or counterintuitive?
   a. We introduced a product or service that flew in the face of the industry norm.
   b. We took exception to standards in our industry.
   c. We wrote about an issue that was grabbing headlines and commented opposite to how most experts did.
5. Do you anticipate questions from the public/media/bloggers/ online journalists and prepare helpful versus hurtful responses?
   a. Sometimes
   b. Never
   c. Always
6. Do you have brand patience?
   a. Yes. I tend to hold back on ideas that don't make sense from a timing perspective.
   b. Sometimes. My executive team or supervisor have advised against releasing a communication due to timing.
   c. No. I send out an announcement just because it gets final approval after several rounds of feedback and edits with no regard for timing.
7. Have you had an open and honest conversation with all departments to decipher when your brand is truly relevant to your audience?
   a. Sometimes
   b. Never
   c. Always
8. Are you and your members on the lookout for strategic alliances to add clout to your PR outreach efforts? Have you made clear what types of things your organization would be interested in?
   a. Yes, we consistently communicate with our key stakeholders what we want our marketing messages to accomplish.

  b. No, we don't communicate effectively or clearly enough how people can help us reach our goals.
  c. We sometimes ask for help with forming alliances and partnerships that will further our mission and vision.
9. If a SPIKE should occur, how confident are you that you would be nimble, could assemble the right team, and get executive, member, and donor buy-in quickly enough to respond effectively?
  a. Confident
  b. Somewhat confident
  c. Not confident
10. Do you test public response in advance and plan platform-specific messaging so you can anticipate a potential issue or opportunities?
  a. Sometimes
  b. Never
  c. Always

Scoring

(1) a. 10, b. 0; (2) a. 10, b. 0; (3) a. 10, b. 0; (4) a. 6, b. 3, c. 0; (5) a. 3, b. 0, c. 6; (6) a. 6, b. 3, c. 0; (7) a. 6, b. 0, c. 5; (8) a. 6, b. 0, c. 3; (9) a. 6, b. 3, c. 0; (10) a. 6, b. 0, c. 5

SPIKE Action Questions

Now what? Consider the following as you read the book:

- Are you going to ask your team to take this assessment at the next staff meeting?
- Are you going to act on this with your next project and tailor it based on your audience's needs?
- When will you schedule time to think about and demonstrate how perfect timing will contribute to the bottom-line and ROI?
- How will you anticipate when you are top of mind—not out of sight, out of mind—for your audience?
- How will you rank the importance of each communications and marketing initiative?

5

Be Nimble, Assemble the Right Team, and Get Buy-In for the SPIKE Method

"Jack be nimble, Jack be quick. Jack jump over the candlestick."
—Midnineteenth-century nursery rhyme

Jack had it right: get over that flame as fast as possible so you don't get burned or, in the case of a SPIKE, get skewered. Interestingly, the significance of jumping *over* a candlestick (rather than landing on top of it and therefore extinguishing it) was good luck for the jumper. Likewise, being nimble in business and in applying the SPIKE method is not merely fortunate it is critical and needs to be planned for in advance. This was never truer than in today's environment of immediate gratification and satisfaction, customization to the nth degree, social media at every turn and on every topic, and so on. The downside for many organizations is that being nimble is the exact opposite of what they are used to and their culture generally allows for. Processes, committees, and drawn-out decision making inhibit change and "nimbility," the ability to be nimble.

In a situation that requires nimbleness, David Meerman Scott, author of *Real-Time Marketing and PR* (2012), said in an interview, "Real-time marketing requires a very different mindset than traditional marketing" (personal communication). Scott recommends taking lawyers' advice with a grain of salt "because their default is to say no to anything that could potentially backfire." Instead, he says,

"Get the legal and the executive team as well as PR in one room and obtain pre-approval for real-time opportunities. It is important that you find good people and give them permission to do their job effectively. Remove multiple layers of approval typically required to get anything done and you will see better, quicker ROI" (personal communication). Maddie Grant, author and owner of SocialFish, spoke to me recently about the notion of being nimble. "Giving your staff, the marketers, and communicators the ability to make decisions quickly, to be nimble, is a core piece of the 21st century culture," she said. This will allow them to recognize SPIKEs and take advantage of them as they arise. "Change has accelerated in the 21st century, and you need to stay ahead of competition, be responsive, be able to ebb and flow with the changes happening around you."

She contends, and I concur, that a major missing component is social media listening. This process of monitoring online conversations is not in marketers' comfort zones yet; they are focusing on more content and more visual, but "are not listening. It's spray and pray," Grant explained. "It's like a smothering mother." That is not to say that companies are not trying. Maddie references an association whose social media manager posts the most retweeted tweet and the most commented Facebook posts into a biweekly e-mail for members. "You have to develop a listening strategy in order to see the trends and patterns," Grant says. These trends and patterns will lead to your discovery and anticipation of SPIKEs. A few online tools that will help you to do this successfully include Hootsuite, Google Alerts, TweetDeck, IceRocket, Topsy, and Social Mention. In addition, the *Huffington Post* recommends several items to set up for automated alerts:

- Your brand name (include alternate spellings or misspellings of the brand names, services, or certifications)
- Executive staff (CEOs, vice presidents of departments, PR staff, and spokespersons, including board members)
- Key messages and phrases commonly associated with your organization
- Event titles (annual conference themes, ideas, and slogans)
- High-profile speakers or people associated with your organization
- Key words relevant to the industry your organization serves

Inherent in social media listening is making it a habit. Have someone committed to this every day and create digestible reports. "It is important to show regular reports, I recommend monthly, to the executive staff," says Grant. "That is the only discernable way to see patterns important for your brand."

Assembling Your A-Team

So, who are the right people to bring to the table when it comes to being nimble? Do you issue a job description for a Director of Nimbleness? A Manager of Quick Action? Coordinator of Agile Behavior? Grant, again, says, "There should be a range of levels and a range of experience. Having the younger and less experienced voice is extremely important. More senior staff can be so ingrained in traditional ways that they don't see the opportunities."

Remember that a chain is only as strong as its weakest link, and if weak is defined here as being less nimble, then you must select at least one nimble person for each department. Additionally, make sure departments know how to work together. Average individuals will make up an average team; staff that is not nimble will add that quality to their respective departments and that quality will flow throughout.

- Look at your organization's mission as a starting point.
- When interviewing candidates, ask them about their own mission and their goals.
- Find out about personality traits and the person's ability to act quickly.
- Set them free. Once you have the right team in place, give them the freedom and trust to do their jobs.

Imagine a chess game as you think about putting your staff together in the best way possible. As Grant told me, "Be clear and transparent with business decisions internally." The size of your staff comes into play here because small-staff associations have an advantage when it comes to acting quickly and creating business strategies, risk factors, and so on. Grant says that playing the chess pieces out comes, by definition, with experience and knowing and understanding the game. You must look for the right people who understand the game and, at the same time, know how to play to the endgame by realizing the opportunity in a SPIKE.

The Buy-In Barometer

There are various levels of buy-in for the SPIKE method at an organization: staff, members, customers, board, chapters, donors, and so on. What level comes first when it comes to identifying SPIKEs and reacting to them quickly? I think it is your staff. Cecilia Sepp, vice president of Association Laboratory, a leading research company based in Chicago, feels it needs to begin internally. "It needs to start with senior staff. They have to make the commitment to nimble communications," she says. Once staff members become true believers, the barometer shifts to the volunteer leadership. "You build questions and critiques into the plan and find a role for the executive committee or board of directors to play," Sepp says.

As you attempt to get buy-in from staff, you need to identify the influencers on your staff and who is being contrarian for the sake of being a naysayer. "Look out for those people and get them on your side in advance," Sepp says. This holds true for your board as well; know who is going to play devil's advocate and ask the difficult questions so you can have your responses ready to go when they hurl them at you.

Additionally, when I spoke to my long-term client and friend Carmenchu Mendiola, vice president of communications at The Washington Center, she talked about buy-in in terms of that ever-present ego and selfishness that seems to always be present in every marketing conversation. "Staff is going to want to know how something affects their department and them personally. If you can position the *so-what* factor in your conversations, that will get you farther. You want to make them look good," Mendiola explains, and goes on to give tips to identify the key influencers as well:

- Who goes to lunch together and who is talking at those lunches?
- Who migrates to the break room at the same time, and who's leading that charge?

- Who rides the train home together?
- Who seeks out whom for the gossip?

Next, you need to obtain buy-in from your board of directors, which will come from the staff selling the idea, and selling it successfully. This can be done by examples, proof that it works, and other "research-based" methods that a board is likely to believe and, thus, approve. The ideas in this book should serve you well as you attempt to gain buy-in from your board.

The next segment for your buy-in barometer, if applicable, is your chapters, regions, and components or special interest groups. They are your global segment, and their reach can be exponential. It is obviously important to get them on board for the SPIKE method.

"Education is huge on SPIKEs and marketing/PR," Sepp explains. "Education helps build the network. I've seen association chapter presidents that can cause a major meltdown when they weren't included in a new process. It is important to recognize that a lot of people don't know what they are doing and others are more sophisticated in marketing and PR. You want them promoting this effort—you are going to double or triple the reach if you are able to educate them and get them to buy in to the SPIKE concept. Communications is not just outreach; it is in-reach."

Checklist for Buy-In

If you want to create buy-in you've got to understand what's in it for whom you are talking to, and one of the most effective ways of doing this is having one-on-one conversations, motivating them to take and pilot new programs. Here's a checklist for buy-in:

1. Open a conversation with staff and ask for their opinion. "Have one-on-one meetings, so you can read their body language," says Mendiola. Don't use e-mail because, as we all know, there is too much room for misinterpretation in this form of communication.
2. Determine the key influencers, and motivate them to talk.
3. Explain how a SPIKE works.

4. Find out who's with you and who's not.
5. Get people to participate in a pilot program for SPIKEs. "There is always someone willing to test an idea," Mendiola says. "Understand that internal ideas are important; the more people are excited about the SPIKE method, the better chance you have at being successful."

Silo Busters

With the SPIKE method, you can break down departmental silos, an issue that runs rampant in associations and has for decades. To create an effective SPIKE plan, use the following outline:

1. Create an overarching objective for your organization's marketing and communications efforts.
2. Break down a list of possible SPIKE projects, events, and ideas.
3. Get each department head to develop a potential SPIKE and to lobby for why their SPIKE is most important for the organization.
4. Each department head should provide a possible scenario and budget with some projected ROI for the SPIKE.
5. If people understand the major organizational priorities, everybody will understand what is truly important from a marketing and communications perspective and put effort behind the "winning" SPIKEs.

Erin Presley, senior vice president of publishing at the National Association of Convenience Stores (NACS), says that breaking down silos all starts with a culture analysis. "The senior staff at our organization has made it a priority to continuously assess how comfortable we are taking risks, making decisions, and killing our sacred cows," said Presley. "We are empowered to make our own decisions and we hold each other accountable on a regular basis. The leadership team meets every Thursday, and we hold quarterly thinking meetings where we read articles, watch an inspiring Ted Talk, have drinks, and talk about what we learned and how we can apply it to NACS."

She explained that NACS focuses on awareness and how to make sure each department and the leadership know what other departments are doing. They meet with key staff to make sure the priorities are the same in all levels of the organization; they are always discussing how to run the association with a business mentality.

"We understand there are certain guardrails we need to adhere to," she explains. "We've always benchmarked ourselves first as a business that happens to reinvest its profits into our industry. That's the nonprofit piece. It is what we do with our profits—the money goes back as a stronger voice for the industry, legislation, products for our members, to freshen trade show."

Presley stresses, "A lot of associations are caught up in the service of members and giving away stuff for free, while for-profit competition focuses on money and time. Associations who have not realized that are not in business anymore. It is kind of late to just now come to that conclusion. It is important to remember that to make change at an association is like 'turning a battleship not a speed boat.' The way we stay competitive is by allocating budget money for people to do some wild and crazy stuff, what we call our disruptive innovation budget." What a great idea!

Ghost SPIKE

However much you can plan and anticipate, you are not a fortune teller and cannot see everything coming down the pike. This book is intended to help you try, but at the end of the day, you may just have to reserve some money in your budget for the unplanned "ghost" SPIKE, an event that happens and that you will need to react to in real time.

Similar to an experimental marketing budget, the idea behind the ghost SPIKE is to have money at your disposal when a SPIKE strikes that you feel is worthy of jumping on. Call it reserves, slush fund, whatever term you want. It's for an experiment, and if it doesn't turn out exactly as planned, you won't be disappointed, because it's in the "extra" column of the budget. It allows for spontaneity, wiggle room, and creativity, within the confines of a solid strategy.

6

Picking the Perfect Audiences and Crafting Compelling Messages

"We often miss opportunity because it's dressed in overalls and looks like work."
—THOMAS EDISON

Sure, spotting opportunity seems like a lot of work, but I guarantee if you and your team review the following items regularly, you can be the first and best at responding to SPIKEs. SPIKEs are your brand's one primary advantage. It's how your brand adds maximum value. It's what makes your brand different and better, and it all centers around timing. Want some good news? There is a replicable process for figuring out your perfect brand moments. And there is no question that when you communicate at the precisely right time, you earn more attention, ROI, and revenue.

Why is timing and using timing wisely so elusive to most businesses? Because, as humans, we are programmed to do things when our instincts tell us to. The only problem is our marketing instincts are often wrong. This is a symptom of being too close to an idea, profession, and problem. We are invested in being committed and consistent with our concepts, past successes, and failures. And we do such a good job of convincing stakeholders that our opinion is right that we are beholden to those ideas, even if they are wrong. Additionally, according to a Forrester Research/Business Marketing Association/Online Marketing Institute survey conducted in 2014, "a startling 72% of surveyed marketers say less than half of their marketing staff plays a primary role in content marketing today—leaving content to quickly degrade to talk of products, features, and what the company has to offer, rather than cleverly packaged bits of the interesting insights buyers crave."

"The gap between content marketing awareness and good content marketing execution is not surprising. It's something we call the digital skills gap," said Online Marketing Institute founder and CEO, Aaron Kahlow, in the release. "There simply aren't enough trained content marketers to do the leg work. But the imperative for education is here and seen across the board, from entry level to CMO" (Levien 2014).

We are trying to decide for the market when we are important to them and when they need us. However, most organizations have a delusional sense of their importance to their audiences. As a PR executive, I hear this sentence more often than anything else: "Why don't more people know about all the important things our organization/profession/brand does?"

Here's the answer: We (consumers and members) don't care unless it pertains to core values, ideas, and problems we are experiencing at the moment. So what affects decision-making, ideas, and interests? You might think that tons of different things affect decision-making, ideas, and interests. You cannot possibly factor everything in, right? Ah, but you can!

Not So Different, After All

Everyone's different, right? We all have individual preferences, history, intent, and relationships with various organizations. Wrong. We all get pop culture, ideas, and inspiration from many of the same places. Be it online news from CNN, *Good Morning America,* blogs, movies, or BuzzFeed, we are all looking at pretty similar information—packaged in different ways from slightly different sources. But, how different? Not much.

Think about this. Your Facebook and Twitter feeds are probably trending the same thing as that of your friend in a similar demographic. If you take a look at critical information from enough varied sources, you can predict what your audience is thinking about. But when creating marketing strategies for their organization, people tend to be too insular. They create content marketing strategies and concepts that would appeal to their own demographic, not to their audiences.

When I was working at Ogilvy before I started my company, I attended a brainstorming meeting about Maxwell House coffee. In the meeting were some young twenty-somethings and a few executives in their early thirties. We were discussing strategies for the famous brand, and I noticed a pattern. Each of the people in the room was in charge of developing concepts that would appeal to their friends, colleagues, and relatives. The only problem was that everyone in the room was college-educated, grew up fairly affluent, and didn't drink Maxwell House—ever. However, I understood the target market because I come from a blue-collar background. My parents love Maxwell House and drink it all the time with their friends. When I stopped everyone from coming up with strategies Starbuck-goers would love, they all agreed they were going down the wrong path and rethought their strategies. Once they broadened their horizons, they came up with winning strategies, because they could put themselves in other people's shoes.

But what if I hadn't been in the room to offer that perspective? Oftentimes, an organization also falls into this very same target-audience trap. The folks on the inside are developing strategies that would work for them, not their target audience. How do you avoid the most common and costly target audience mistake?

Here are a few things to consider:

1. **Picking your target audience is the first and most important step to any initiative.** If your target audience is wrong, everything else will be wrong too. It is a domino effect. For instance, if we continued down that path of Maxwell House with a Starbucks customer in mind, the ideas would have fallen flat, felt wrong to the audience, and the timing of the message would have been off. Don't let that happen in your organization. Guard your target audience like that first cup of coffee you drink each morning.
2. **Determining your true target audience takes work.** Have you given it enough thought? Do you look at objective data or data that supports your previously held beliefs? Do you pick one audience to focus on or are you trying to appeal to everyone with the same message, timing, and ideas? Pick a lane.

Read that again. Pick a lane and stick to it. It is so important to focus your efforts. Don't try to appeal to everyone—because you'll wind up appealing to no one. Target audience selection, environmental scanning, and listening online and off are critical skills for your organization's success.

3. **Picking the right channel is critical.** This is based on demographic research. As Gary Vaynerchuk, author of *Jab Jab Jab Right Hook*, says, "Context is king"; but I would say, timing is king. In his book, he suggests people consider "social marketing is now a 24/7 job" (2013, 27). I contend that if the context is right but your audience isn't ready to receive your message, you can easily create dissonance and disengagement for your brand. Without the right timing, the best message on the most appropriate channel will still get ignored.

Don't Forget Traditional Media

The first channel people select is some social media channel, but research shows that traditional media is still the most influential. In *Contagious: Why Things Catch On,* Jonah Berger found that social media yields only 7 percent in word-of-mouth marketing for a brand (2013, 11). Seven percent. That is so small that social media should be one of the last tactics you turn to to build consensus and interest. There are so many tactics and strategies to choose from it can be overwhelming. Whether it's an executive visibility campaign, media relations, SEO, advertising online or off—take the time to deep-dive into all the tactics and strategies at your disposal and think about social media *as a support.* I know that is so counter to what others are saying, but I'll say it again: SEVEN percent! That is astounding.

That said, having a well-managed social media presence does need to be an integral part of your brand strategy, especially if you are using timing and SPIKEs for your brand. Being at the right place at the right time will increase people's interest in getting information on your social media pages, especially if they are on target and on time. But if you abuse the goodwill of your tribe by posting or retweeting irrelevant stories, you run the risk of a 7 percent engagement in word of mouth.

One example of using social media as support is my friend Brian Carter, best-selling author of *The Like Economy*. He is a social media expert and uses his Facebook advertising campaign to draw interest in traditional media outlets to have him appear as an expert on MSNBC, CNN, and Bloomberg TV. Isn't it interesting that social media experts flaunt traditional media appearances to help prove they are credible? Think about that for a while next time you want to do a complete social media campaign without other tactics in mind. I'm not saying not to utilize social media; I am saying to do what works for your audience, when and how they want to hear it.

What Your Audience Wants

Compelling messages that are short and counterintuitive. A perfect example of a message that cuts through the clutter is the Stand Up to Cancer campaign. One of the organization's key messages is "This is where the end of cancer begins." Repeatable and memorable, the message offers a different twist on cancer and cancer research than any other organization before it. The proof point the organization uses is equally powerful: "1 in 2 men and 1 in 3 women in the U.S. will be diagnosed with cancer in their lifetime. We're investing in the future of cancer research, bringing new treatments to patients faster."

Another example is the Ban Bossy initiative by LeanIn.org and the Girl Scouts. The website, http://banbossy.com, brilliantly explains the position with this statement:

> When a little boy asserts himself, he's called a "leader." Yet when a little girl does the same, she risks being branded "bossy." Words like bossy send a message: don't raise your hand or speak up. By middle school, girls are less interested in leading than boys—a trend that continues into adulthood. Together we can encourage girls to lead.

As a proof point to support why people should ban the word "bossy," they use this statistic: "Between elementary and high school, girls' self-esteem drops 3.5 times more than boys.'" Again, these messages are very memorable. For a guide on how to test your messages, review the questions at the end of this chapter.

Well-spaced messages. Your audience can only absorb so much information at one time. If your marketing team is overloading them with information that is only relevant to your organization, your audience will begin to tune you out. Because many organizations work in silos and one hand doesn't know what the other hand is doing, many messages are duplicated. Avoid this by having a "What Not to Put Out" list of items for e-mails and social media messages. Giving staff guidance on what not to put out is more effective than telling them what they can create, post, and share.

Bite-sized chunks of data. If you can, provide data in small chunks to add to the coverage of an issue. The media, bloggers, and websites love visuals that are sharable. Micro-sites, myths versus facts, infographics, and bits of information that are relatable and repeatable are vital to your organization's success. If you can't relay the most important research, findings, and data to your next-door neighbors without them furrowing their eyebrows, mystified by what you are saying, "you haven't passed the eyebrow test and your message needs work. Your messages and proof points are confusing and are not helping you tell your story more effectively," says Sam Horn, the author of *POP: Create the Perfect Pitch, Title, and Tagline for Anything.*

The Convention Industry Council's "Economic Significance Study of Meetings to the US Economy" showed that the meetings industry is actually larger than the auto industry. As discussed in chapter 10, the US meetings business supported 1.7 million jobs and generated $263 billion in spending in 2009, according to the study released by PricewaterhouseCoopers. Not only was the message and research perfectly timed (the value of meetings was in question while the automotive industry was receiving a large bailout from the US government), but the information was presented in short, easy-to-grasp infographics.

Tasteful messages that aren't opportunistic. Be forewarned: being opportunistic can actually harm your brand and bring more criticism of your marketing and PR efforts. An example of a brand with the worst opportunistic social media gaffe has got to be Kenneth Cole. During the Arab Spring in 2011, the company released a tweet that said: "Millions are in an uproar in #Cairo. Rumor is they heard our new spring collection is now available online."

Wow. It is poor taste to try and capitalize on other people protesting about freedom. Seriously, what were they thinking?

Groundhog-Day Your Messages

No matter what type of influence strategy you use, your messages must be concise, repeatable, and memorable. A great way to do this is to repeat, repeat, and repeat the message again and again.

In the movie *Groundhog Day* Bill Murray's character repeats the same day over and over again: he is woken up by an alarm clock that plays Sonny and Cher's famous song "I've Got You Babe"; he bumps into an old classmate before stepping into a pothole, and he reports the news regarding the famous groundhog's shadow at Gobbler's Knob. Anyone who has ever seen the movie can remember these details vividly, even if it has been 10 years since the last time you've seen the film. That brings me to what communicators can learn from this cult classic. Throughout my career, I've always been astonished when I've read most corporate communication messaging documents. They are difficult to remember, filled with jargon, and most important, they are not repeatable. Whether it is for the launch of the new product or a standard way to talk about an organization, I almost always see the following mistakes:

- The sentence structure is complicated.
- There are too many messages.
- The messages use words people would never say in a conversation.
- The choice of spokesperson delivering the message is rarely taken into consideration.

To see whether your organization's messages pass the test, take a cue from the movie *Groundhog Day* and see how many people can repeat your messages aloud. For additional testing, try these techniques:

- Get the corporate communications team or agency who wrote the messages to test them on camera. If they can't remember them or use them in 60 seconds, the messages do not work.

- Do a focus group or on-the-street interviews and ask people to repeat what they learned about your company when you recite your messages. See what sticks. If they can't remember them, go back to the drawing board.
- Tailor the message *slightly* for each spokesperson to ensure that each person's cadence of speech, word choice, and style is taken into consideration.
- Choosing your messages is the art of sacrifice. In the end, you should only have three to five messages and supporting proof points.

Writing prosaic prose may be the dream of many would-be creative types posing as PR professionals and corporate communication staffers, but in the light of day crafting messages that are repeatable is the mark of a true communications guru.

Messages and Audience Exercise

1. Who are your top three audiences? Create messages to match their needs, desires, and pain points. Focus on your next 100 customers or members you want to attract and prioritize audiences accordingly.
2. Would someone actually say the message you have on your website or in your marketing or PR materials? Practice by saying your message out loud.
3. Does your message reflect the tone, cadence, or style of the person delivering it? Train your spokespeople with the messages and adapt them to meet each person's speech pattern.
4. Are your messages clear, concise, and repeatable?

Remember, it's about when your audience wants to hear from you and when your voice can be the most effective.

Manufacturing a SPIKE

Provide First-of-Their-Kind Pitches, Stories, and Messages

*"The greatest problem in communication is the illusion
that it has been accomplished."*
—GEORGE BERNARD SHAW

To understand timing and to maximize the times when your organization is most top of mind to your audience, you must do environmental scanning regularly. According to Business-Dictionary.com, environmental scanning is defined as "careful monitoring of an organization's internal and external environments for detecting early signs of opportunities and threats that may influence its current and future plans" (www.businessdictionary .com/definition/environmental-scanning.html). I've read many books and have heard countless experts say you need to have your PR, marketing, and social media team tethered to all the channels you participate in 24/7/365. That is a crazy expectation to put on anyone, and it is also not realistic. You may be saying, "I can't add another thing to my plate—it is already overflowing." If you want to stop the marketing madness, then adhere to following the six options for manufacturing first-of-a-kind pitches, stories, and messages for your organization with a critical eye, and everything else will fall into place.

In any business, industry, or profession, there are telltale signs that indicate when your company, cause, or creation experiences an uptick in interest (good or bad)—your SPIKEs. You just have to know what to look for. And this requires a level of skill that most companies assign to the most junior person to analyze. Therein lies the opportunity. If instead of an inexperienced person doing this, you and your senior management team divide this list of critical items to scan, you will come up with brilliant strategies to get ahead, predict market opportunities, and seize the day. The trends, ideas, and opportunities will materialize before they are in the public purview.

The News Cycle Has Flipped

In the past, mainstream media was the catalyst for public conversation. If you saw something on the nightly news or in the *New York Times*, you would talk to friends or family and that's what helped spark public conversation. But, there's been a shift in how topics become popularized. The public, with access to social media platforms, are now in many cases the ones driving conversation. In many instances, the news cycle has completely flipped.

Although journalists have always looked for new sources, angles, and story ideas, they are now using the public to provide what has traditionally come from press releases, events, and insider sources. Because journalists get better story assignments, promotions, and placement based on how shareable and clickable their stories are, they're now looking to bloggers and the general public to provide them with content that will get people talking. **Social media and bloggers are a great testing ground. What better way to tell if something will be clickable and shareable then to look at what people are already saying?** If journalists can make a topic broader to appeal to a mainstream audience, they have a predetermined topic that will get people fired up and talking back.

This is a huge opportunity to manufacture SPIKE opportunities by staying ahead of issues. If you can figure out how to get in the ground floor of a topic, instead of trying to pitch an idea after a story breaks, you'll be the go-to source. Don't wait for them to spot the story—help them out by pitching a story about what's already bubbling up.

To do so, you must pay close attention to bloggers, people on social media within your industry who are starting rumors about an issue, person, or cause. These posts may seem insignificant, even annoying perhaps, but they represent a viewpoint others are too scared to share. Pay attention to their opinions or watch them seep into trade and national media in a relatively short time frame. Check out figure 7.1, which shows the buildup and build down of a SPIKE.

For bloggers, the post has to be presented in a way that draws people in and makes them click. Therefore, consider bringing in an opposing viewpoint to the blogger's post. For instance, if the blogger took one stance, you and your members or customers take another. If you know others are listening, trade or mainstream media for instance, you can use this as a way to draw attention to your perspective, position, or SPIKE. Pitch the opposing viewpoint and watch your e-mail box explode with interested journalists who want to capitalize on the conversation.

Additionally, you can write about nuances, quirks, and information that may surprise people on your blog and link them to the comments section of the trending blog or social media platform. I've had clients do this with great success, even being quoted on CNN, Mashable, and TechCrunch because they added to a story already picking up interest. This is a successful, and relatively easy, way to manufacture a SPIKE for your organization.

What's Trending?

Another option is to look at *Good Morning America, The Today Show,* CNN, the *New York Times,* Facebook, and Twitter, which all have mechanisms you can follow to see what the world is buzzing about or, as they couch it—"what's trending." This gives you inside information for what the media are about to expand on from a reporting perspective. Additionally, you are given a great opportunity to pitch and create resources that expand on the current pop culture obsessions. From movies to award shows, you can piggyback in real time on the excitement and coverage that these events bring.

Think about how the *trending story* may develop and whether it pertains to your organization's core mission and brand promise. If you think it falls into your brand's zone of influence, think like a journalist by looking at the facts collected about the story and

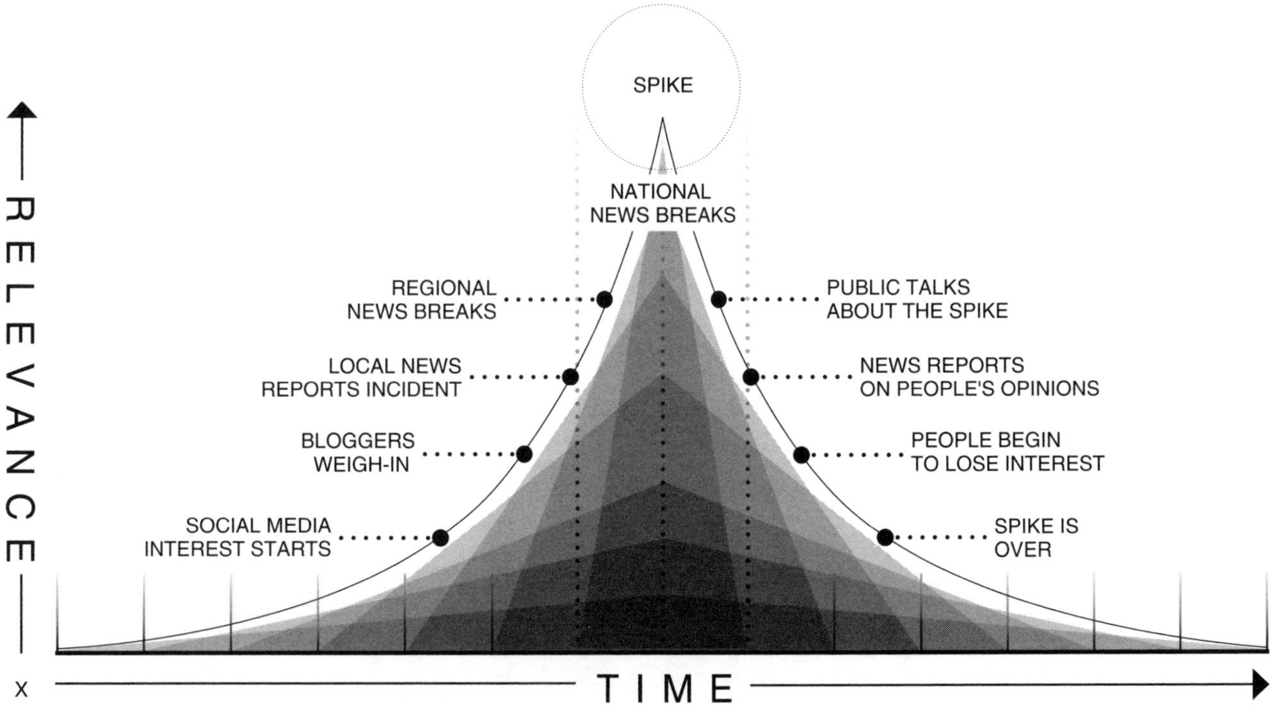

Figure 7.1. The Buildup and Build Down of a SPIKE. *Source:* Courtesy of Epic PR Group

what you might be able to add to the conversation. For an interesting and unexpected angle, create a pitch with the *opposite* of where your pitch will end. As an example, if you are the American Medical Association and there is a story that is trending about a new healthcare law, make your pitch all about how the medical profession will be positively affected by the changes. Then, however, turn the tables with a twist by arguing that the way the rest of the media are reporting the story is missing critical information. What's more, you and your organization's members can provide commentary on the correct outcome. This will surprise journalists and get them to call you for your point of view.

Check out the free website, http://buzzsumo.com/. Basically, it's Google for what's trending. Just type in a keyword, and it will tell you what articles, posts, and tweets are being shared and by how many people. This will also help you uncover patterns for what will work for your target audience. For instance, are they more likely to share a post with 5, 15, or 20 tips? Check out behavior patterns in your target demographic, which will help you unlock what it takes to get your content trending, too.

Awards, Celebrities, and Grabbing Some of the Fame

The Academy Awards, Grammys, MTV Music Awards, and Cannes Film Festival are all great opportunities to hitch your brand to a winner. The greatest opportunity for brands lies in the spaces between—that is, the show before the show and the show after the show. Media love to draw out award shows, repackage clips, and create b-roll about how the night unfolded. Is there an award-winning movie, song, or event that talks about your company, industry, or profession that you should respond to or acknowledge? Do so before or after the award show and you are likely to get maximum engagement online and off. The media will want to interview you, and your social media friends will want to share your in-depth perspective. Be sure your members are media-trained and ready to create a SPIKE.

Let's say a celebrity takes a position, does something thought-provoking or gossip-worthy on a topic close to your organization's bailiwick. You may be able to jump on their success and add to yours. Remember, people pay attention to what their favorite pop star, actor, or reality show celebrity says and does. Even if they don't give it much credence, they are definitely paying attention at that moment. Capitalize on it to educate and to inform them.

Or, say, an artist, actor, or business executive is on meteoric rise. The rise and fall of any star gets people talking. Consider the fall of Donald Sterling, the infamous owner of the LA Clippers, who was caught on tape making racist remarks. If you are an organization or association that deals with race-related issues or diversity, there has never been a better time to talk. Yet, few organizations have the resources or ability to respond quickly enough to be a key player in the news coverage and social media conversation. Why not? They have to know that someone somewhere will eventually say something outrageous like Sterling, so why not prepare to be top of mind when the public is most interested in hearing a balanced, educated opinion on such a hot topic? Ask these questions:

- Would your organization be able to make such a difficult decision under such intense external scrutiny? If not, you must prepare to do so in the future.
- What are your organization's hot-button issues?
- What positions do you stand firm on as a group?
- How would you respond if those values, ideas, or positions were put to the test?

If you are not sure about any of those, find out. Or risk missing opportunities or getting pulled into a viral spiral, which can make your brand vulnerable and ruin your reputation. Contemplate having a board retreat to decide where your organization stands before an issue becomes too heated to touch.

Competitors, Allies, and Relevance, Oh My!

A major incident happens directly related to you, your organization, or cause. A competitor widely known for supporting one thing takes a position or stand that doesn't make sense and is inconsistent. That is your opportunity to spring into action. How exactly do you know what opportunities require your response? That is precisely the conversation you should have before those opportunities arise. And you know what they are. Spend some time prioritizing widely spread myths or misconceptions about your organization among competitors or naysayers. Rank them according to importance and discuss which issues you would want to take a stand on.

Remember to keep close tabs on the allies in your industry or profession. If they make a misstep that is widely reported and opposite of your organization's position, say something. Don't let the opportunity to be heard when members most need to hear from you pass you by because you are too busy answering e-mails and attending meetings. These are golden SPIKE opportunities.

If you and your organization are on the more cautious side, wait a few days, max. After the reporting is under way is the time to take a stand. Look at the coverage timeline and see where your subject matter experts can add credibility and build out your position. Waiting too long may make your opinion unreportable.

Predicting What People Will Argue About

Although celebrity pundits may draw boos and hisses from people across America, they are effective at catching people's attention and unleashing viewer emotions. So, what's got the political pundits talking? Consider how you or your company, cause, or creation can add to their fury and fodder. Go where the loudest, most influential talkers are and build your case around why their argument doesn't hold water and use it as a platform to gain influence. Soon, people will be turning to your content to discover opinion. People love to have something fun to say at a cocktail party! An e-mail newsletter called theSkimm gives people a list of things they should say in different situations, pertaining to breaking news. In one issue, theSkimm has a section on "What to say if someone asks if you are jetlagged" and they give a tongue-and-cheek response based on the Secretary of State and how much he is flying as a result of the Israel crisis. What if you could do that for your association?

Talking heads like Bill O'Reilly, Lou Dobbs, and Geraldo Rivera score among the most influential people in America, according to an article by Tom Van Riper, a *Forbes* magazine staff writer, and a poll conducted by E-Poll. Others included on that list should be Jon Stewart, Howard Stern, Anderson Cooper, Greta Van Susteren, and Maureen Dowd. The emotional connection these folks have with their viewers is an important signal of what people care about—and piggybacking on an emotional pull works. Use it to your advantage when they are spouting off about things that are important to you and your organization.

Presidential Initiatives, Press Conferences, and New Laws

If the president of the United States supports it, talks about it, or proposes legislation or a program you should pay attention. What the president says does matter and matters to many people in your organization and outside of it. Understand that any time the POTUS speaks or provides press conferences, it's time to listen. See if your issues are presented. If so, don't miss an opportunity to be heard. It doesn't even have to be a political response, but it should be something that shows you get it. Also, other media will report on what the president says, which gives you and your brand and your experts a national media platform to comment.

For example, in July 2014, President Barack Obama spoke out against "corporate deserters"—a term he used to define companies who are setting up headquarters overseas in order to avoid America's high corporate tax rate. During a speech in Los Angeles and an interview with CNBC, the president said it was "unpatriotic, comparable to renouncing one's citizenship, and harmful to the U.S. economy for businesses." While not directly calling out any specific companies, Obama said the whole of corporate America "cannot focus only on the capitalist pursuit of higher profits … Companies taking advantage of current loopholes want the advantages of doing business in America without paying their fair share" (Wolfgang 2014). Strong words and strong feelings across the aisle, for sure. However, whether you wholeheartedly agree, vehemently argue, or just plain don't care about this statement, if you are with the American Institute of CPAs or any one of the 50-plus state and regional societies that serve certified public accountants, this is a news item that you can jump on. This could bring a SPIKE to your organization simply by being in the know and disseminating the information, showing you care about your constituents. On the other hand, the American Association of Individual Investors (AAII) may have a 180-degree take on the news and Obama's position, but that organization has an equal amount of opportunity to manufacture a SPIKE by reporting on the speech and interview (just as the AAII's more than 20 chapters across the country do).

If new legislation is passing and it affects your members or customers, you should keep your ears open and respond as changes pass and the law evolves. This is such a missed opportunity for many organizations whose public affairs or government relations department work without coordinating with the communications and marketing staff. Be sure to prioritize legislative issues your organization will respond to and inform your members about.

Don't wait until your association's fly-in to debrief them on all your work. They are too overwhelmed to absorb what you are telling them as they grace the steps of Capitol Hill. Instead, offer updates only when critical measures will affect your members and their business or profession. Be selective about the updates and vigilant about what needs member or customer attention. Be on the lookout and keep your PR ears to the ground for any and all political, legislative, and presidential announcements that can SPIKE interest or conversation for your organization.

What Brings In the Most Revenue?

If you are still trying to figure out what to focus on for your organization, then focus on the programs, products, and services that bring in the most revenue. This may seem too obvious, but in fact it may be difficult to see for people in associations and nonprofits because they are mission- or cause-driven. If most of your revenue comes from a certification program focused on hazardous waste cleanup, then focus on when the general public is interested in hearing from experts in this field, such as after an oil spill or when a story breaks related to repercussions from fracking. SPIKE the story and have experts and content on the ready.

It's important to remember that marketing still needs to complement and support the organization's revenue goals, so if you are searching for ways to manufacture SPIKEs, look at what your customers, donors, and members value most about what you offer and use the described formula to develop ideas that will catch their attention and improve bottom-line numbers.

8

When Is Your Brand Truly Relevant?

Turn Your Editorial Calendar into a Relevance Calendar

"I've learned that people will forget what you said, people will forget what you did, but people will never forget how you made them feel."
—MAYA ANGELOU

Relevance is defined as having direct bearing on the matter at hand; being pertinent. In many instances, we are trying to create interest around things that are outside our brand's circle of influence. The SPIKE technique is news-jacking on steroids. Instead of just jumping on the news bandwagon, we'll teach you how to lead the pack when it is most critical for you to be heard.

Don't just settle for commenting when the media and your followers expect you to—break through the noise with the element of surprise. Understand the current trends, peaks in interest, and general discussion about your industry, profession, and company. This is often a very predictable pattern year after year, once you can understand when others (media, customers, members) are already thinking about your brand. As suggested in chapter 18, too, use the element of surprise to your advantage. Send out a pitch, idea, or post that will raise eyebrows.

For instance, if you are a fitness expert, you are probably well aware that there are myriad stories that will come out in January about New Year's resolutions. Surprise your fans, followers, and the media with a pitch or content marketing piece on January 17.

Why? Because that is the day most people give up on their resolutions, according to an article by Melissa Burkey, PhD, in *Psychology Today*. (The day has even been dubbed "Ditch Your New Year's Resolution Day.") Taking advantage of this type of knowledge and combining it with timing manipulation will gain you widespread attention because you're bucking the trend, and the media will love it because it is a headline in the making.

Be Aware: Don't Do It When Everyone Else Does

Let's examine the American Speech-Language-Hearing Association (ASHA). The association's members are audiologists and speech pathologists. Seemingly, National Autism Awareness Month in April each year would be the perfect time to demonstrate the association's tools and resources for speech therapists that treat autism. But think again. Parents aren't actually thinking about ASHA during the month of April. They think about how to address the issue as the issue becomes top of mind for them—not during an awareness month. (I'll explain in more detail how to think through relevance differently.) The truth is parents, healthcare providers, and media are looking to expand the autism story and get more detailed information after the month has passed. ASHA should consider when its members need resources from them, not when it's most convenient for the organization. If they can understand when parents are most engaged with solutions and are looking for additional materials, ASHA can use timing as a differentiator to fill in the autism information value gap for their members.

Why? Consider all the other organizations competing for their attention related to autism: Autism Speaks, Autism Society, Autism Research Institute, Organization for Autism Research, National Autism Association, American Autism Association, Autism Society of America, US Autism and Asperger Association, National Autism Center, Association for Science and Autism Treatment, not to mention a host of state associations. All those associations and nonprofits, along with for-profit products and services, are trying to communicate with industry influencers like parents, teachers, and healthcare providers during April on social media and traditional media.

Is that the best use of ASHA's resources, time, or marketing efforts? Will ASHA experience maximum attention ROI, or will their voice just be drowned out in a large chorus of more relevant players? Of course, the answer is the latter. ASHA would be more impactful and beneficial for its members *leading up to* April or *right after* the National Autism Awareness Month. And if they use that timing, there's even better news. Those other autism-related organizations have primed the "interest pump" for ASHA. Think about it. It takes a while for those other organizations to build awareness. When April ends, the content, coverage, and noise related to the issue dies down, but parents' interest in and research on the topic is at an all-time high. It's top of mind because it's been so noisy all April.

ASHA's height of influence and impact is not during an awareness month, which is an easy strategy that isn't as effective in today's fragmented media environment. In addition to right before and right after the awareness month, perhaps another viable opportunity for ASHA to raise awareness is right after parents receive their autistic child's first progress report at school. This timing would seem to prompt a parent to seek a speech pathologist's advice to address the speech issue. Another option on timing may be as the summer rolls around. This is logically the time when a majority of parents begin thinking about enrolling their child in a class to set them up for success in the next school year. The point is that timing—timing that really cuts through the clutter—requires more strategy than before, and brand managers and executives need to demand better for their organizations.

Timing is also the best differentiator for ASHA and other organizations looking to create awareness. Why? Because ASHA can become an authority by picking a time to communicate. Typically, marketers release information when they are ready, not when the target audience is ready to receive it. This is a huge oversight for traditional and media initiatives, but social channels are only making this more apparent. Content may be the new black, but timing is still king.

If content is not delivered *when* a brand's target market is *ready* to receive it, content marketers could create an avalanche of ill will or inaction. In my experience, timing is one of most essential elements to consider in any campaign, but this is where many marketers fall short.

Aim Right and Hit Your Mark

Let's take Target as another example, in the wake of its credit card catastrophe in late 2013. As a company, Target didn't consider its current state of affairs and its strategy simultaneously. As I am writing this book, Target has 22.7 million Likes on its Facebook fan page. As the retailer undergoes the largest data breach investigation in history, Target's content marketing strategy seems somewhat schizophrenic.

The brand's page goes from telling fans how to throw the best Super Bowl party to how Target's CEO is participating in a hearing on Capitol Hill to protect consumers. I'd be willing to bet a hefty sum that the content Target is currently sharing is automated and *timing* wasn't even factored into the posting equation.

If I was one of the millions affected by the breach, I'd be pretty upset by Target's flippant approach to dealing with the gravity of this issue. It seems like the social media, content marketing team, and PR team didn't communicate. I know this is controversial to say, but I believe content and content curation should be the primary job of the PR team, with other teams acting as support including customer service, IT, and content marketers. PR people are most qualified to spot brand relevance, deal with issues quickly and effectively, and activate a brand campaign when needed.

Pure and simple, if brands don't pay attention to timing, a skill that is born and bred in most PR people worth their weight in salt, they will lose the attention, and more important, the respect of their followers if they continue to churn out content for content's sake. In the wake of a crisis or as a brand's perception shifts, brand managers should stop yelling into their own noise and turn their automated editorial calendars into relevance calendars.

Consider the following multipronged approach to create relevant content, with timing being a paramount underpinning to the strategy:

1. Rock the brand relevance calendar. List when your brand can be most impactful. Be merciless in your evaluation of what is relevant and what is not. One of our clients is an intern organization called The Washington Center (TWC). We know, and they know, that they are most relevant in the summer months when interns invade Washington, DC. For 40 years, the organization focused on relaying the importance of its academic programming, not the brand experience. Carmenchu Mendiola, the vice president of communications, was determined to help make the brand cooler and sexier. She hired Epic to help her develop a concept that would take the organization to the next level. We decided to start by listening, finding the gaps, and understanding what interns were hoping to get from an internship organization, besides beefing up their resume. Resoundingly, it was the lack of respect of employers, Washingtonians, and businesses that really stirred emotions in interns and got them angry. We knew it was an opportunity to create a SPIKE for TWC. Knowing this emotional trigger was a very important element in creating a campaign that not only the interns would talk about, but area businesses as well. Together, we created InternsRock, a week-long celebration of the 20,000 interns that descend upon DC each summer. For the initiative we created a brand partnership with mtvU, Macy's, and Gap.

The concept was covered by every major news outlet locally, including the *Washington Post,* the *Washington Examiner, The Hill,* and several local broadcast channels along with tons of blogs and websites. Here's what Wonkabout, a famous Capitol Hill blogger, wrote about InternsRock week:

> Seriously, if you're an intern and you don't take advantage of this deal, you deserve every mean/rude/scandalous thing that has ever been said about you. This is an excellent opportunity to experience DC in a way that most young professionals can hardly afford to.

The campaign was a great success among students. It provided discounts and deals at local eateries, bars, and coffee shops and the whole city rallied around InternsRock, while TWC became the go-to source for interns around the city. The point of this story is that the organization realized when it was most relevant and capitalized on that timing. We created a stellar campaign around when the organization had the most influence and relevance among its main target audience—interns.

Figure 8.1 shows how much impact the campaign had for the organization.

Figure 8.1. The Washington Center's InternsRock Participation Infographic. *Source:* Courtesy of The Washington Center

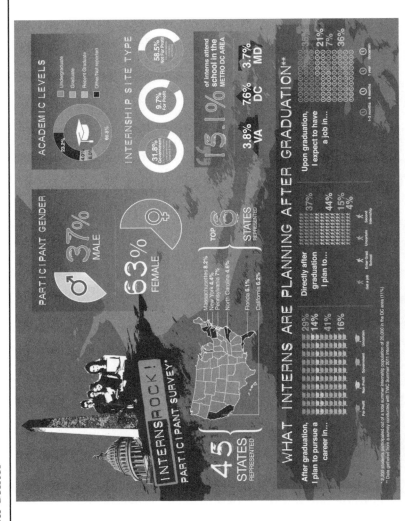

2. Create a timing twist chart. Understand when people are expecting to hear from your company, cause, or creation. Then, buck those trends and surprise them with an interesting twist from a timing perspective. If you have a female audience and you do your real-time promotion during the Super Bowl, you can dwell on the fact that many women aren't tuning in and use that to your advantage. In fact, many women are using their second screen device such as an iPad or smart phone looking for content that interests them.

For example, Carters, a clothing line for kids, did a Super Bowl halftime sale online, which was brilliant. Because I am not a football fan yet still wanted to watch the big game to be with my husband and friends during that time, Carter's Facebook marketing promotion worked! Why? Carter's target audience, moms, were actually watching the game, not for the game but for the social aspect, including the halftime show, commercials, or promotions. Of course, I was watching the game, but not closely, and had my iPad in my lap, scrolling through my Facebook feed. Carter's target audience was present on Facebook and, therefore, tuned in to the marketing message. But be forewarned. It can actually harm your brand and bring more criticism if your marketing effort feels opportunistic.

3. Find the influencers. I mention this in many chapters in this book. Why? Because it is extremely critical in creating, recognizing, and maximizing SPIKEs. In every industry there are influencers; these are the people who are leaders, trend-setters, and go-getters, the folks we all know and reference as thought leaders. If you are looking for a shortcut, there are software tools such as Cision that can help you determine media influencers in your industry, but you shouldn't only look to media for thought leaders.

- Research who's speaking, writing, and leading the organization.
- Pick the top 25 people to target and find a way to introduce your brand with a WIIFT (what's in it for them) approach.

Keep in mind that it is critical to explain the benefit to the influencer. The worst is when I get an invitation to "partner" with a company with no explanation as to why I should spend my time helping this company get noticed. If I'm influential in the market, that's one thing and that's a benefit to them. What is in it for me? Never forget to tell them why knowing you will help them.

4. Make ideas steal-worthy. Let's face it. There are no new marketing ideas. The truth is that not everything you do has to be absolutely 100 percent original. It just has to be an original version for your market, industry, or profession. See what has worked for other companies and associations and create something similar for your market. For instance, Taco Bell recently did a campaign where they sent out "breakfast phones" to 1,000 food bloggers in order to get them to blog about the fast-food chain's new waffle breakfast taco. When I saw this idea, it immediately got my creative juices flowing, so I created a similar concept for the association market.

Let's be clear. Association executives aren't known to be fast-food lovers, or food bloggers, or even in the same target demographic as Taco Bell's (males between the ages of 18 and 24). However, the (taco) shell of the idea was there, and that was enough to get people talking. I remade the idea and its ingredients and called our campaign #EpicBuzz. We selected 50 association influencers, all who were people other people trusted, respected, and listened to in the association community. Just like Taco Bell, we bought burner phones (throwaway cell phones) and mailed a phone to each of our influencers, then launched the campaign around the ASAE Marketing Membership and Communication Conference (MMCC), where I was speaking and exhibiting at a tradeshow booth (see figure 8.2).

The campaign was a perfect SPIKE for my business because we used the phones to create challenges, dares, and funny stunts to get our influencers talking at a show that a majority of my prospects were attending. The campaign worked and garnered more than 326 tweets in two days, 60 of which were pictures of the influencers, and drove 400 potential clients to our booth. We weren't launching a product like Taco Bell; we were simply trying to build brand recognition and gave out some cool prizes in the process. We were hands down the most talked about company at the tradeshow. What idea inspires you? Make sure you take the elements that will work for your company, cause, or creation and adapt them as needed.

Figure 8.2.   Epic PR Group's #EpicBuzz Influencer Phone Campaign.   *Source:* Courtesy of Epic PR Group

5. Use the multiplier effect for influencers. In *Word of Mouth Marketing* (Sernovitz 2012) author and marketer Andy Sernovitz, references what Potbelly Sandwich shop did to get people talking, and he calls it "the multiplier effect." After I read Sernovitz's book, I realized that I do this for my campaigns without knowing what it was called, and you should, too. Here's how it worked for the now national sandwich shop. When Potbelly's opened its first shop in Austin, Texas, they rented a mailing list that included a list of all the people in Austin who had just moved there from Chicago. The handwritten letter said:

> Congrats on your recent move! I hope you are settling in and enjoying Austin. But, I must ask, are you a little homesick? We are thrilled to bring you a taste of home by opening a Potbelly in Austin.

Enclosed you'll find ten free sandwich tickets, our gift to you, to help you share the Potbelly love with your friends.

The smartest part of the campaign was the 10 sandwiches, which got people sharing, talking, and getting their friends to go to the new shop with them. Brilliant. What can you learn from this sub sandwich shop? Understand what experiences, ideas, and products people want to share with others and don't overcomplicate things.

Having the structure, resources, and team to react and become top of mind when it matters most should be the top priority for any organization. Effective convergence for an organization relies on the creation of a primary list of ways in which you want to be relevant to your audience. Remember, it's easy to follow the pack. But using these timing and relevance twist techniques to stand out from the crowd is what will set you apart.

9

Brand Patience

Why You Need It

"Patience is power. Patience is not an absence of action;
rather it is 'timing'; it waits on the right time to act, for
the right principles and in the right way."
—FULTON J. SHEEN

The *absence of action* requires impossible feats of self-control for the most seasoned executives and marketers with all the channels, platforms, and methods available to communicate a message. Yet the most powerful brands, the ones with the most impact, seem able to practice this restraint. They wait for the precisely right time to act. They understand when real-time marketing makes sense for what they are trying to communicate. They also pick the right channel to communicate that message most effectively, even if it occurs within a situation of immeasurable sadness.

The American Academy of Pediatrics (AAP) released information on how to talk to children in the wake of a tragedy after the mass shooting at Sandy Hook Elementary School in Newtown, Connecticut. AAP felt a sense of responsibility to offer support and resources during such a horrific loss. And, at the same time, AAP allowed consumers to see the value of what they do as an organization. On December 14, 2012, twenty school-age children were shot and killed by Adam Lanza, the son of a teacher at the school (Barron 2012). Parents everywhere were left crippled by the reports of what Lanza had done and perplexed at the thought of explaining such a horrific incident to their children, who would invariably hear the news.

Parents and teachers across the country tried to make sense of Lanza's shocking and devastating actions and were faced with having to explain and answer questions about the Sandy Hook shooting to their students and children. Almost as soon as news of the shooting hit national media, AAP was issuing a statement from its then president, Thomas K. McInerny, MD, FAAP, on its website and to the press with links to information on how to talk about disasters with children ("Pediatricians Can Offer Care for Grieving Families after the Loss of a Child" 2012). McInerny and AAP's quick response got the statement and press release picked up and shared throughout regional and national media across the United States and instantly positioned AAP as the go-to resource and expert for parents and teachers on how to communicate with children about the school shooting.

Statement in Response to the Elementary School Shooting in Connecticut

12/14/2012

By Thomas K. McInerny, MD, FAAP, President, American Academy of Pediatrics

Today is a day of sadness and grief for everyone who cares for children. The American Academy of Pediatrics (AAP) offers its deepest sympathies to everyone affected by today's tragedy at Sandy Hook Elementary School in Connecticut. Pediatricians and other child health experts strongly recommend that schools and parents avail themselves of resources to help them talk with children about this disaster. As in any frightening situation, young children should not be exposed to the extensive media coverage of the event—in other words, turn off the TV, computer, and other media devices. The AAP offers resources for talking to children about disasters, and advice on watching for signs of stress and trauma. Parents also can use their child's pediatrician as a source of advice and support during this time (McInerny 2012).

After speaking with Dr. McInerny, I learned that AAP's media presence was secured long before the tragedy in Newtown. The organization regularly reviews and releases policy updates on various issues and conducts annual press tours with the acting AAP president. And every year AAP releases about 60 statements on various health and safety policies for children. Each statement is researched and updated every three to five years. AAP's mission, "to attain optimal physical, mental and social health and well-being for all infants, children, adolescents and young adults" ("AAP Facts" n.d.), positions them as a thought leader on all things kid-related.

AAP's position statement on firearm safety had been updated and released in November 2012 in what would be an uncanny, yet fortunate, chain of events for the organization's communications strategy.

> A month or two before the Newtown tragedy, that [firearm safety] statement had been fairly researched and was a very well documented statement about firearm safety; we could rely on that as something we can turn to and immediately make available. We have a superb team ... that is able to work with the media on all kinds of issues, including responding to disasters, so we activated that team very promptly. We let out press releases and statements that were issued to the press and the media that were favorably received and helpful in getting a message across to not only the families of Newtown, but to the rest of the country as well. (Thomas K. McInerny, telephone interview, 2014)

Had AAP not laid such a solid foundation for its policies through well-cultivated and groomed media connections and contacts, it may not have risen above the noise during such a chaotic event. The goodwill created by this type of SPIKE has a "long-term brand value for AAP and gives us an opportunity to help people when they need us the most," said Dr. McInerny. AAP's serendipitous release on firearm safety just a month before the Newtown tragedy, paired with its network or media contacts, created a SPIKE for the organization and solidified AAP's position at the top of its industry.

Even though AAP releases those 60 statements each year, that does not mean it has 60 SPIKEs in a year. In fact, Dr. McInerny said, "AAP has no idea which statement will bring in the most media attention." AAP became the expert source for the Newtown shootings not just because they had a policy statement on firearm safety, but because they had a communications strategy in place and were ready to react when the organization's SPIKE was occurring.

Not only was it the right thing to do, a source of comfort and a reassurance for parents, but AAP became a resource for a multitude of issues because they seemed to "get it" in the media's eyes. That is, something simple, easy to share, and smart. Some may say that this was just a one-in-a-million chance, but it was much more than that. It was smart planning that required an outward perspective on when an organization is relevant. The AAP isn't a consumer-focused organization typically, but in this instance they knew its members could provide a valuable service to parents in need of guidance. And the media responded in kind. Because of AAP's words of wisdom, traditional and online news outlets such as ABC News, CNN, PBS, *USA Today,* the *Huffington Post,* the *Washington Post,* and the *New York Times* pointed to AAP as the go-to resource, and links to the organization's website were included in articles about the Sandy Hook tragedy.

Moving forward, and probably for a very long time, parents, teachers, and concerned guardians will turn to AAP for research and information. Moreover, the trade and consumer media is also now going to pay attention to information released by the AAP because the organization showed that it understands its expertise and can be relied upon to provide information when the timing is right—externally.

Controversy Can Mean Constructive

No matter where you stand on gun control, the way the National Rifle Association (NRA) responded to the Sandy Hook shootings was perfectly timed. It can be a lesson for other organizations on the controversial end of an issue, which inevitably will happen— perhaps not of these proportions, but it will happen nonetheless. The NRA's response is an illustration of a well-planned PR response when the organization was up against an incredibly emotional audience. For gun enthusiasts, the NRA needed to demonstrate support, but walk a fine and careful line with sensitivity, given the weight of the situation for parents everywhere.

According to the *Washington Post,* the NRA remained silent for a week after the incident and held a press conference on December 21, 2012. The NRA recommended that armed guards be placed at elementary schools nationwide for protection against such shootings (Sullivan 2012).

At that time, Wayne LaPierre, executive vice president of the NRA, said, "Out of respect for the families and until the facts are known, the NRA has refrained from comment. While some have

tried to exploit tragedy for political gain [referring to people calling for harsher gun laws], we have remained respectively silent.
Now we must speak for the safety of our nation's children" ("Remarks from the NRA Press Conference on Sandy Hook School
Shooting" 2012).

He further went on to explain how the media would portray
the NRA's position: "Now I can imagine the shocking headlines
you'll print tomorrow. More guns, you'll claim are the NRA's
answer to everything. Your implication will be that guns are evil
and have no place in society, much less in our schools. But since
when did 'gun' automatically become a bad word. A gun in the
hands of a secret service agent protecting our president isn't a bad
word. A gun in the hand of a soldier protecting America isn't a
bad word. And when you hear glass breaking at three a.m. and you
call 911, you won't be able to pray hard enough for the gun in the
hands of a good guy to get there fast enough to get there. So why
is the idea of a gun good when it is used to protect us . . . but bad
when it is used to protect children in schools?" ("Remarks from the
NRA Press Conference on Sandy Hook School Shooting" 2012).

Let's dissect why the NRA's messaging and timing were effective. Think about how coordinated the NRA must have been to
stay virtually silent for a week as pro–gun-control groups slammed
them in the media. That level of coordination comes with a lot of
practice dodging controversy.

If your industry or profession was attacked, how easily could
you assemble and contact similar groups to remain united in your
approach? This stance helped the NRA talk about something that
was still in the interest of its members without vilifying gun owners.
If the NRA responded right after the tragedy, that would have put
them directly up against parents, kids, and all those in mourning.
Instead, the NRA helped shape its side of the argument through
appropriate timing.

Many times people focus on the speed with which companies
or associations respond to a crisis, but in this instance, patience
paid off and allowed them to build a strong argument, not seem
defensive. Instead, the NRA waited, listened to the gun-control
advocates, and chose to speak when it was the right time to
be heard.

Timing may seem like common sense, but many organizations, especially associations, get this wrong. Many organizations don't take the time to consider when they might be relevant externally.

One Size Does Not Fit All

It is important to realize, however, that not all brands or associations should respond to an issue as sensitive as the Sandy Hook shootings. Most notably, the American Counseling Association, the American School Counselors Associations, and the National Association of School Psychologists all responded to that same incident with a list of resources. Why, then, did AAP have the most success? It was because it was most appropriate for AAP to weigh in, given the situation. The organization represents the largest group of people parents would turn to in this situation, and the fact that they had just released specific research related to the incident all factored into AAP's success. They weren't opportunistic or self-aggrandizing; they were human in their approach and announcement, and because they had established relationships with key members of the media before the situation arose, they were able to contact those reporters and build on the organization's credibility.

Apology Trifecta and Video Addresses

Although Ralph Waldo Emerson said long ago that "nothing astonishes men so much as common sense and plain dealing," it never ceases to amaze me that CEOs and their PR teams do not think about who in charge should be accountable in a crisis. Without accountability, the public feels as though nothing will change. Now, sometimes that requires the company or spokesperson to take more than their fair share of the blame. Therefore, shooting, editing, and designing a personal video address that includes an apology from a designated spokesperson may be necessary should the situation escalate.

Be sure to consider the spokesperson's demeanor and how they will be reported, including their body language, tone, and attitude. As a former reporter, there was nothing I disliked more than someone who talked down to me when they were in hot water. That created ill will and, like it or not, impacted how objective I was able to be. If you have someone who seems ill-equipped to deal with tough questions or folds under pressure, rethink the spokesperson or get them media-trained immediately, before feeding them to the wolves, that is, the media.

We've encountered some that don't want to be in a position to advocate for one member over another. If that is the case, consider tapping into your board president or PR team or hire a paid spokesperson to do the video response and subsequent interviews. Be careful, because if this is not done well, the media, stakeholders, and others will use the video to demonstrate how out of touch the organization is with the situation at hand.

Rather than addressing the actual cause of the criticism, apologizing, and clearly stating how they plan to rectify the situation, companies or associations sometimes focus on unrelated positive aspects of the organization. Mentioning previous philanthropy and social responsibility can certainly be important aspects of effective crisis messaging. However, it does not negate the crucial need to directly address the cause of the crisis.

There are three vital steps to an effective apology—the trifecta:

1. Apologize without a caveat.
   a. Hands down, this is one of the most common mistakes leaders make in a crisis. They recognize the need to apologize but dilute it with a clarification or by placing blame on others. Instead, keep the apology simple, pure, and genuine. Then focus on the solution.
   b. Domino's did this right. After a video of Domino's employees tampering with pizzas went viral in 2009, the CEO apologized and took immediate action to correct the misconduct (York 2009). Period. End of story.
2. Acknowledge the human impact.
   a. Whether it involves layoffs, personal injury, or catastrophic harm, every crisis affects people personally. Do not ignore this. By showing sympathy, leaders are seen as acknowledging the gravity of the situation. BP ignored the human impact entirely. Instead the CEO said, "I'd like my life

back" (Durando 2010). In a few short words he made the crisis much, much worse. People didn't need another reason to dislike BP, but the CEO certainly gave the public one more reason.

3. Pledge a solution and stick with it.
    a. When you emerge from a crisis with a solution, make sure you can live with the positioning strategy for a long time. With BP's dark website (see chapter 20) and consistent disaster response efforts, the company won back some goodwill. Like BP, your organization must be able to see a strategy through to ensure that the negative impact to the company or association is lessened with the content provided on a consistent basis.

To Respond or Not to Respond: Key Questions to Ask Yourself

1. Is your organization really the best source for the story?
2. Can you think of someone else who would be better than you? Why or why not? Use the *why not* to consider the pitch.
3. Consider your primary audience and whether this issue relates to them enough to take a stance or position or to comment. You don't want to alienate your most important stakeholders, just to make a point.
4. How much value would you be contributing to the conversation? Would it be substantial or insignificant?
5. Put on your reporter hat. Would the media expect to hear from you on this issue, or would they be surprised?
6. Think about whether your comments and research would amount to a feature article or a mention. If a mention, you probably want to refrain.
7. Is there anyone who is comparable to you that has already commented on the issue at hand? Do you have a different perspective that is worth pitching in a time of crisis?
8. Look inward and make sure you are truly aligning the mission and goal of your organization with the issue or crisis at hand. If not, you could be perceived as opportunistic.

SPIKE Spotting

"PR cannot overcome things that should not have been done."
—HAROLD BURSON, cofounder of Burson-Marsteller

Many organizations and businesses try to attach themselves to real-time events that make no sense for their brand, product, or market position. There is a famous example of a real-time social media response strategy by Oreo, during Super Bowl XLVII. When the lights went out in the stadium, the snack food capitalized on the viewership and opportunity for exposure with a tweet that said, "You can still dunk in the dark."

Why did it work? Because a snack food is something we talk about and pay attention to during the Super Bowl. It was Oreo's SPIKE, but no one asks what the cookie did the rest of the year. Why? Because it doesn't matter. That one SPIKE had a far greater payoff than Oreo's actual Super Bowl ad, which cost millions more to create. It's not enough to just get a viral spike—you have to know how to be prepared to take advantage of the success of the campaign. What is your equivalent of the time at which you are most relevant? When is your industry or profession's Super Bowl moment, and how do you prepare? With a dedicated team to respond to issues as they happen, it will be the best ROI for the dollar you spend all year. Be prepared when you are most relevant.

In order to predict a brand SPIKE with some degree of accuracy, answer the following questions. This will help you to identify key opportunities where you can plan for brand SPIKEs, good or bad.

SPIKE Spotter: Predicting a Positive Brand SPIKE

1. Do you take full advantage of the most critical time to communicate with your organization's main audience, or have your communications and marketing strategies fallen short due to repetition or lack of interest from executive or marketing staff?
2. What external factors or upcoming changes in legislation, regulation, or perception would impact your ability to deal with a crisis or opportunity?
3. When does your audience expect to hear from you (annual conference, earnings, end of the year recap, and so on)?
4. Have you set aside budget, time, and resources to respond and be nimble when a positive or negative SPIKE occurs?
5. How would you spot your ideal SPIKE? How would you best describe your unique timing, benefits, approach, products, service, or position in the market when that SPIKE occurs?
6. Rank your ability from 1 to 5 to be the best resource for a topic. Think about how you can improve that ranking with new or current research, position papers, timing, or by following news stories and media trends and forecasting legislative opportunities.
7. What might trigger a response in your industry that even internal and external stakeholders would recognize as an opportunity for your organization to be part of the conversation?
8. Have you given stakeholders a description of the perfect industry SPIKE? In our experience, yes, and so specifically that when a SPIKE does happen, I have several people in my network alert me to comment. I ask people to look for companies or high-profile individuals who are either thriving or just surviving a crisis.

9. What is the biggest vulnerability your industry, product, or service may face in the next six, nine, or twelve months?

10. In recent history, what has been the worst external-facing crisis that brands in your industry have faced, successfully or unsuccessfully? Were you prepared or did you comment? How quickly were you able to react?

Anniversaries, Office Moves, and Promotions

Most organizations focus on when they think they are having a milestone event such as moving offices, executive promotions, and anniversaries. Truth be told, I hate when organizations focus on these types of events, because no one cares but people in the organization. That's right, I said it. You know you've always wanted to say it, too.

We once had a client celebrating a 50th anniversary for their association try to spend $250,000 on an initiative to drive awareness for the organization. Guess what? That was the complete wrong way to use that budget. It was setting the board, organization, and members up for failure and ridiculous expectations riding on one campaign to represent the brand and its history. Wouldn't it be better to focus those resources on small campaigns and initiatives over time? Of course. Not to mention, what happens when the anniversary year is up? Nothing, zilch, nada.

Although I understand that some of these announcements need to be made, I would refrain from spending a huge amount of budget to promote them. Have a party, put out a press release, and move onto important issues that address your customers' needs, not your organization's.

What Most People Do Wrong with Awareness Months

Awareness months can be tricky from a timing perspective.

Too many organizations that have **indirect ties** to an awareness cause send out information before or after it is relevant to their organization. Only use awareness month marketing when you can be a majority voice, not a minority stakeholder of influence.

Don't waste a SPIKE on a time when you aren't supposed to be talking. People will get sick of hearing from your brand.

New Data and Research

As new data and research are released, people who are close to your brand, as well as those outside of it, are more likely to shift perspectives. Use this opportunity to couch the information in an accessible manner. Most organizations and businesses I work with make data unmanageable and, worse, inaccessible to those outside the organization. The information is so nuanced, granular, and specific that it gets lost. Consider how your industry, profession, or business changes will affect everyone else.

Make sure that data is also reflected in your findings. For instance, as mentioned earlier, we worked with the Convention Industry Council (CIC) on the "Economic Significance Study of Meetings to the U.S. Economy," and the most compelling data and message point that came out of the findings were that meetings surpassed the auto industry in creating jobs in the United States. That is an incredible statistic and should cause a shift in how people think about the meetings industry at large. We made sure that specific message point was pulled out and backed up with findings. CIC now has a statistic that makes the meetings industry relevant to everyone. By practicing brand patience, discussed in chapter 9, CIC can wait to create a brand SPIKE by arming themselves with this information and rereleasing the data at a time when "jobs" are a hot topic (see figure 10.1).

Revealing Data in an Exciting Way

Step 1. Consider what data you have and how it relates to the current climate. You don't need to release all of your data at once. You can make it available on your website, but release statistics when they make sense for your organization.

Step 2. Be strategic about timing. If you have data that could be relevant throughout the year, think about when your information most relates to your audience's current interests and use that as an opportunity to create a SPIKE.

Step 3. Showcase your data in a compelling format. Small bits of information that are displayed in an interesting way are more likely to be shared across social networks.

Figure 10.1. Convention Industry Council's Meetings Mean Business Infographic. *Source:* Courtesy of the Convention Industry Council

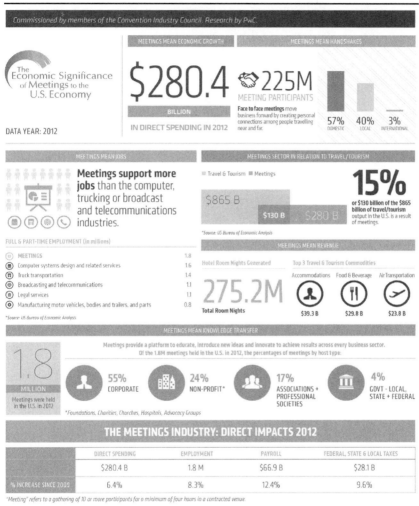

Commissioned by members of the Convention Industry Council. Research by PwC.

The Economic Significance of Meetings to the U.S. Economy

DATA YEAR: 2012

MEETINGS MEAN ECONOMIC GROWTH

$280.4 BILLION
IN DIRECT SPENDING IN 2012

MEETINGS MEAN HANDSHAKES

225M MEETING PARTICIPANTS

Face to face meetings move business forward by creating personal connections among people travelling near and far.

57% DOMESTIC   40% LOCAL   3% INTERNATIONAL

MEETINGS MEAN JOBS

Meetings support more jobs than the computer, trucking or broadcast and telecommunications industries.

FULL & PART-TIME EMPLOYMENT (in millions)

MEETINGS	1.8
Computer systems design and related services	1.6
Truck transportation	1.4
Broadcasting and telecommunications	1.1
Legal services	1.1
Manufacturing motor vehicles, bodies and trailers, and parts	0.8

Source: US Bureau of Economic Analysis

MEETINGS SECTOR IN RELATION TO TRAVEL/TOURISM

Travel & Tourism   Meetings

$865 B
$130 B $280 B

Source: US Bureau of Economic Analysis

15%
or $130 billion of the $865 billion of travel/tourism output in the U.S. is a result of meetings.

MEETINGS MEAN REVENUE

Hotel Room Nights Generated

275.2M
Total Room Nights

Top 3 Travel & Tourism Commodities

Accommodations   Food & Beverage   Air Transportation
$39.3 B $29.8 B $23.8 B

MEETINGS MEAN KNOWLEDGE TRANSFER

Meetings provide a platform to educate, introduce new ideas and innovate to achieve results across every business sector. Of the 1.8M meetings held in the U.S. in 2012, the percentages of meetings by host type:

1.8 MILLION
Meetings were held in the U.S. in 2012

55% CORPORATE   24% NON-PROFIT*   17% ASSOCIATIONS + PROFESSIONAL SOCIETIES   4% GOVT - LOCAL, STATE + FEDERAL

Foundations, Charities, Churches, Hospitals, Advocacy Groups

THE MEETINGS INDUSTRY: DIRECT IMPACTS 2012

	DIRECT SPENDING	EMPLOYMENT	PAYROLL	FEDERAL, STATE & LOCAL TAXES
	$280.4 B	1.8 M	$66.9 B	$28.1 B
% INCREASE SINCE 2009	6.4%	8.3%	12.4%	9.6%

"Meeting" refers to a gathering of 10 or more participants for a minimum of four hours in a contracted venue.

Convention Industry Council 700 N. Fairfax Street, Suite 510, Alexandria, VA 22314
For more information on the study, go to www.economicsignificancestudy.org

 MEETINGS MEAN BUSINESS

SPIKE Spotting

In my experience, it is remarkably harder for for-profit organizations to come up with new concepts because there is typically more competition and budget dollars being spent on marketing to get noticed, especially in burgeoning markets. The quickest way to get noticed is to create trends from concepts that are already spiking in a variety of industries, which can be supported by anecdotal research and data. Although developing trends may seem difficult, I've provided three examples of trend frameworks, which can be used to develop trends in any industry.

One of the easiest trend frameworks is what I like to call the time machine framework. The setup is deceptively simple:

- In the past ...
- Now ...
- Where your trend will take people, products, service, industry, and so on ...

As an example, here is the time machine framework in use:

- In the past, companies have opened up some of their products to crowdsourcing.
- Now, a step above crowdsourcing, customer-controlled innovation allows your audience to take part in the creation of actual products, services, and changes to the company.
- As a result of the Crowdsourcing 2.0 trend, the customer-company dynamic has changed as it becomes clear the best way to ensure customer satisfaction.

Next is the what's cool framework. Everyone wants to be in the know and this creates the perfect way to draw people in.

- Everyone is doing it because this is what the consumer desires ...

As an example, here is the what's cool framework in action:

- Facebook was cool ten years ago.
- Phone calls are for old people.

- E-mail is for parents.
- Now, the *visual social trend* is in with the popularity of Pinterest, Snapchat, and Instagram.

Another trend framework that is used in a variety of industries, especially luxury-related industries, is the scarcity trend framework:

- The trend has been bubbling up for a while ...
- What others didn't do until now ...
- Research shows ...
- How the trend will address a need for a select group of people in the know ...

As an example, here is the scarcity framework in action:

- First propelled into the urban consciousness by New York's Magnolia Bakery in 1996 and subliminally promoted by the pleasure-seeking women of the HBO series *Sex and the City*—cupcakes have always had a place in our heart.
- Businesses such as Sprinkles Cupcakes and Crumbs continue to draw repeat customers who appreciate the dessert's size and portability.
- When an economy enters troubled waters, this does not spell bad news for all categories. "Affordable luxury," for example, tends to perform well in a recessionary environment.
- Given the recent economic downturn, Georgetown Cupcake sells out its treats with a long line of patrons waiting to buy the $2.75 cupcake because people feel "it's an affordable luxury."

These trend frameworks will help any company manufacture concepts that keep the organization current and fresh based on real-time market wants, desires, and anecdotal data.

Begin by reviewing and understanding what experts say is coming next in your company's industry. Look to publications such as *Harvard Business Review,* the *Atlantic,* and the *New Yorker* to see what is starting to pick up interest with intellectuals. Additionally, look at the polls and surveys from industry experts. Many times, the conclusions of the data tell you something about what experts are looking to find.

For example, let's say social media experts are currently developing polls and surveys to support the idea of the benefits related to data analytics. This tells me that developing data that refutes those polls or puts varied information together from other industries in a surprising way will drive attention to my brand. It is all about how you package new polls, research, and information.

Moreover, while I am reviewing new data, I am always listening to what people are talking about around the water cooler and at parties. Social media is no substitution for this. What gets people talking online is what they want to project publicly—being at a party gets people to be forthcoming in a way that is uncommon online. This is still a great method to understand what really gets people talking.

SPIKE Spotting for Nonprofits

I work a great deal with associations and nonprofits, and although each one has different audiences, issues, and goals, there are many commonalities that make SPIKE planning similar across all. For example, nearly all associations have an annual conference, a board, a distinctive brand, and a budget planning season. Here are some things to keep in mind throughout the year that can help set you up for successful SPIKE spotting.

Annual conferences. Your annual conference is an important time to connect with members, existing and prospective. However, for prospective members, they are not likely in membership "buy-mode" while they are there. Review membership data from past years in relation to the annual conference and determine when the typical prospect is in "buy-mode." Dedicate resources to the months following the annual conference to engage prospects and stay top of mind following the annual conference, just after you've demonstrated your value.

Board meetings. Use board meetings as an important tool in your SPIKE planning. By understanding the issues that are currently of concern to the board and to the industry, you can better spot opportunities to create your own SPIKE or identify one. Board meetings are a great place for active listening. As issues are reviewed, get a sense for how the room is responding and feeling about each issue—try to pick up on the issues that get a lot of buzz going in the room. If your board is buzzing, you know members will be too. Use board meetings as a test ground for a larger campaign. Preview the campaign to the board or a committee to gauge response and adapt as necessary.

Changes in leadership, platforms, and brands. Change is difficult, and it's important when introducing a change to your audience that you plan for both good and bad SPIKEs. Current members, prospective members, and the media are all important to consider when introducing change, whether it's a change in leadership, member dues, branding, or taking a different stance on a particular issue. When planning for an announcement, keep in mind that although a SPIKE is likely to occur, have multiple plans in place for navigating through your SPIKE, depending on your audience's reception. I would argue with some early audience listening, you should be able to gauge the type of SPIKE you will have. But never assume. Don't take it lightly and be inclined to think all will go well. Do your homework, listen to members, and learn about how they talk about your association.

Budget season. During budget season, meet with fellow departments and understand their priorities for the next year. Piggyback on their big initiatives and listen to your audience to determine when it makes the most sense to draw attention to a particular project or cause.

Fundraising push. Increasingly, organizations that directly ask for fundraising dollars are at a disadvantage. This should make nonprofits rethink how they spend public relations dollars. The 2014 ALS Ice Bucket Challenge is a good example of the changing landscape. Since the ALS Association began tracking the campaign's progress on July 29, 2014, it has raised more than $53.3 million from 1.1 million new donors in what is one of the most viral philanthropic social media campaigns in history, according to an article in the *Huffington Post* (Lauckner 2014). This campaign was fun and engaged people in all walks of life, including celebrities who joined in the fun. What other organizations can take from this challenge is to create campaigns that are easily explained, doable for every age demographic, and use social proof. People who were asked by others to do the challenge were publicly called to the task or asked to donate to the association. Social proof is an excellent motivator for people and should be incorporated into each donor push.

11

The Upshot of a Positive SPIKE

"The opportunity to secure ourselves against defeat lies in our own hands, but the opportunity of defeating the enemy is provided by the enemy himself."
—SUN TZU

Sun Tzu, famous for writing *The Art of War,* is correct. All you need to create an opportunity for your organization is to listen closely, analyze openings, and pounce when the perfect SPIKE comes along. That raises the question, "Who is listening for your SPIKE, trends, or opportunities on the horizon?" Have you assigned arguably the most important job at your organization to an internal researcher, junior marketer, or social media expert? Is that the most objective person for the job? Or are they simply looking for ideas that support what your organization has always known to be true? It's worth investing the time and resources into hiring an outside researcher or senior marketing or PR professional to discern patterns and opportunities with a critical eye. When you have someone in place who can look for opportunities, it's equally important that you have a plan to ensure you can maximize your SPIKE when the time comes.

Take a Public Stance and Become a Go-To Expert

To spot your SPIKE and raise it even higher, you must first describe your perfect opportunity to your audience and followers, both online and off. If you make yourself an expert on a topic or create a public stance on an issue, not only will you have someone you've paid looking out for your opportunity to SPIKE; you'll also have loyal brand supporters who know what you're interested in and can help you identify and maximize it. For instance, there are a number of people and brands that rally their tribe when they need help or support for an issue they've identified as their area of expertise. Vani Hari is known as "the Food Babe," and she and the Food Babe Army have literally taken some of the biggest corporations in the food industry to task through organized online protests, rallies, and viral campaigns. Chick-fil-A, Chipotle, Kraft, General Mills, Subway, and Panera have all been subject to the Food Babe Army's scrutiny.

In a recent example, Hari and her loyal followers discovered that Subway allegedly had a potentially harmful chemical, azodicarbonamide, in its bread (Hari 2014a). According to Hari's website, her army started a petition and garnered 50,000 signatures in 24 hours, voiced their concerns on Subway's Facebook page, and refused to buy their products until changes were made in the bread's ingredients (Hari 2014b). She started a hashtag #nowaysubway and shot a video on her own web channel, Food Babe TV, which explained that the chemical was not used in other countries, only in the United States (Hari 2014a). In less than a day, Subway agreed to remove the chemical and completed this change as of April 2014. Over 450 news stories covering the Subway investigation and online petition were aggregated on Google News (Hari 2014b).

Headlines included (Hari 2014b):

- ABC News—Subway takes chemical out of bread after protest
- USA Today—Subway to remove chemical from bread
- NY Daily News – Subway will remove additive found in plastics from its bread after blogger's online petition
- CNN—Meet the "food babe" who helped convince Subway to remove chemical from bread
- Canada CBC News—Subway agrees to end use of controversial chemical after food blogger Vani Hari's protest
- Late Night With Jimmy Fallon—Subway Yoga Mat Controversy

Clearly identify issues that are emotional in your industry and take a position. While you may not need to be as extreme as someone like Vani Hari, you can take a stance on something.

Ignite Brand Loyalists and Draw Attention to Your Campaign

If you clearly identify your brand's strong position on an issue or expertise on a topic, you can find opportunities to SPIKE and create a campaign around it. Activate your members by providing clear action steps such as signing a petition, sending letters to legislators, participating in social media conversations, and informing traditional media of the issue. It is much more powerful for a group of people to take a stance. Use their interest to build momentum for similar issues moving forward. The Human Rights Campaign (HRC) did an incredible job when they decided to change the color of their logo from a yellow equal sign on a blue background to a pink equal sign on a red background. They asked supporters of marriage equality to change their profile pictures across their personal social media platforms to the new logo.

What was initially a small part of a large campaign to raise awareness of the upcoming Supreme Court ruling on California's gay-marriage ban and on DOMA, the Defense of Marriage Act, went viral. Facebook estimates nearly 2.7 million joined in changing their profile picture to the new HRC logo (Colgrass 2013). Everyone who shared the new logo made a public stance to their own social media following, creating new HRC supporters in the process.

Another clever way the HRC kept people interested and engaged in the passing of the legislation was a direct mail campaign. The HRC sent holiday cards to supporters, showing which states were voting on the law. This sent out a signal to people who lived in those states to raise their voices as the legislative issue was approaching.

TD Bank is another great example of a company creating a SPIKE and generating brand loyalists. On July 24, 2014, TD Bank

Canada released a video of how they say "thank you" to their customers (TD Bank 2014). The video showed customers at an ATM, typically known as an automatic telling machine, which had been converted into an automatic thanking machine. The ATM then began to personally thank TD Bank customers with money, prizes, gear, and trips. A mom was given money to invest in her children's future as well as tickets to take them to Disneyland. Another mother was given tickets to Trinidad to visit her daughter ailing with cancer, and a lifetime Toronto Blue Jays fan scored gear, met his favorite player, and got to throw out the first pitch at a ball game. TD Bank created a positive SPIKE by giving their customers personalized experiences that they are going to talk about for the rest of their lives. Creating brand loyalists is not only about building a camp of devoted followers but getting them to talk about you to others and build out your audience through sharing tales of goodwill.

This is when brand nurturing makes the most sense. *Brand nurturing* is the idea of treating a brand like a living thing. A trendy idea, nurturing only works when people want to engage with the brand and the issue is something your organization feels passionately about. Don't waste your audience's time with minor issues with little or no impact.

Make It Easy for Others to Help Elevate Your SPIKE

In the example of Food Babe Vani Hari, her ability to rally her troops has made her the go-to source on topics such as GMOs, labeling, and food investigations. What can you learn from this food expert and online consumer advocate? Plenty. Her messages are clear, short, and thought-provoking and her content is easily shared. Take Hari's hashtag created for her Subway petition: #NoWaySubway. It rhymes and it's easy to remember. Her Facebook page is visual, and every piece of information is sharable and general enough to be adapted to the sharer's opinion and stance on the issue. In addition, her online petitions are easy to use, and quickly shared with the click of a button. She is able to get her army to react quickly, and she follows through with her message until the company gives in, providing regular updates and showing how companies react to her claims, extending the life of her SPIKE. Moreover, she offers her followers a form e-mail that can be directly sent to a company's CEO and other members of leadership. Here is a sample of the e-mail form letter created for Subway, care of Hari's website (Hari 2014a):

Dear CEO Fred DeLuca, Head of Global Marketing Jeff Larson, and Director of Operations Joe Chaves,

Azodicarbonamide is a chemical used "in the production of foamed plastics." It's used to make sneaker soles and yoga mats.

It's also used in almost all of your Subway sandwiches, is banned across the globe, and The World Health Organization has linked it to respiratory issues, allergies and asthma. Some studies show that when heated, azodicarbonamide turns into a carcinogen.

We ask you to remove azodicarbonamide from all Subway sandwiches, and make your bread just like you do in other countries. We deserve the same safer food our friends get overseas.

We want to really "eat fresh", not yoga mat.

Sincerely,

[Your name]

If you are looking to rally your members or customers in support of an issue, Hari outlines a format that will get people talking online and off and will trigger interest from top-tier media. She lets the Food Babe Army do the heavy lifting and creates a bigger voice for herself in important conversations related to food.

The Girl Scouts, in partnership with LeanIn.org, put in place a campaign called "Ban Bossy" to help girls feel less self-conscious about being leaders. The microsite about the campaign provided audience-specific messages that explained the organization's position on the word *bossy*. Organizers made content specific to various audiences such as young girls, parents, teachers, managers, and Girl Scout troop leaders and encouraged those groups to share their custom message. It is such a smart move because the campaign incorporates word-of-mouth marketing as well.

Tip Off the Media to Your SPIKE

Another interesting phenomenon is how engaged traditional media gets with these types of initiatives. I refer to this as the "media echo chamber." A great example of this was the viral Kony video, produced by the charity Invisible Children (2012). It spread across the web like wildfire, as the charity hopes to bring Joseph Kony, the Ugandan leader of the violent, child-recruiting Lord's Resistance Army, to justice. The viral film, with over 100 million views to date, was even given an official accolade by the White House on March 8, 2012 (Epic PR Group Staff 2012a). The sheer popularity of this viral campaign compelled hundreds of media outlets to cover the issue.

However, at the same time, the campaign has also invited criticism against Invisible Children. Skeptics and activists alike have voiced concerns about the methods used by Invisible Children, its allocation of funds, and the idea that the video promotes *slactivism* (the self-deluding idea that by sharing, liking, or retweeting something, you are helping out). Regardless of where you stand on the video, it provides an interesting case study for the media echo chamber we see between traditional media and social media.

The relationship between traditional media and social media continues to evolve, a symbiotic connection that fuels viral SPIKE campaigns like the #StopKony initiative. We call it the "media echo chamber" because a story echoes from social media, to traditional, back to social (and may not always happen in that order).

Is an online trend truly indicative of what people really care about, talk about, and think about in real life? Or is it just a way to kill time during the day and make yourself appear altruistic? How many *Kony 2012* tweeters, sharers, and likers will actually engage offline?

The answers to those questions will vary depending on whom you ask, and it also remains to be seen how many #StopKony supporters will actually get involved offline. But it's clear that some stories echo louder than others—meaning, they jump from social to traditional media easier and more quickly than others. So what makes a story more likely to be in the media echo chamber? There are a few key things:

- **Sheer mass of interest.** Widespread online conversation, celebrity support, shares, clicks, and likes.
- **Numbers.** The video has been viewed more than 100 million times.

- **A human element.** The Kony video is human-interest at its core, not just by disparaging the cruelty of Kony himself, but also by highlighting the love and hope filmmaker Jason Russell has for his own son to grow up safe and free.
- **Controversy.** The video campaign is certainly not without controversy and criticism. Skeptics, fact-checkers, and traditional media outlets question Invisible Children's accuracy of information, organizational model, and allocation of resources.

It goes without saying that the Kony video is the perfect storm of the media echo chamber.

We Have the Right to SPIKE

That said, how do you know when the right moment will create a positive SPIKE for your organization? It has to feel so right that it would actually be wrong not to comment. It's go-with-your-gut. But remember that the moment has to be closely tied to your brand, your position, and unique selling proposition. Many organizations that get this wrong don't seem nimble or agile; they just seem opportunistic. When a brand gets a positive SPIKE right, it is celebrated online and off.

A recent example is Arby's tweet to Pharrell Williams about the hat he wore to the Grammys that looked remarkably similar to the brand's famous logo (see figure 11.1).

Arby's tweeted to Pharrell with this message: "Hey @Pharrell, can we have our hat back? #GRAMMYs." The tweet earned more than 83,000 retweets and was favorited over 48,000 times. Arby's social media manager Josh Martin says it has garnered 10,700 replies and helped the brand win 6,000 new Twitter followers, according to a blog interview with MarketingLand.com. Additionally, Pharrell Williams also tweeted back to Arby's, a clear win for Arby's on Twitter, because the singer and rapper has 2.7 million followers. Other brands like Quaker Oats, Pepsi, and Hyundai chimed in to support the fast-food chain's win (Gesenhues 2014).

How prepared are you to recognize positive SPIKEs at your organization? According to an interview with Martin, his CMO gives him the freedom to capitalize on opportune moments that

Figure 11.1.   Arby's Famous Hat Logo. *Source:* Courtesy of Arby's

make sense for the brand. "Our CMO has created an environment for our team to have freedom and flexibility," said Martin in the interview with MarketingLand.com. "I'm not going to put the brand in jeopardy. If I do think it's controversial, I run it up the flagpole." Martin says "the free range he has gained comes from building trust with his supervisors over time" (Gesenhues 2014).

How trusting are you with your staff to capture a real-time moment for your organization's brand? Do you have a clutch player on your marketing team that will take the reins and seize the moment? Take the advice of Josh Martin at Arby's and give your marketing folks the range to be widely successful by maximizing real-time opportunities using the SPIKE method. Hats off to your association if you don this SPIKE successfully.

Finding the Lost Principle of Influence

"Public opinion is a permeating influence, and it exacts obedience to itself; it requires us to drink other men's thoughts, to speak other men's words, to follow other men's habits."
—WALTER BAGEHOT, British journalist,
businessman, and essayist

When creating and launching a new product, service, or brand, you must always weigh whether the change will produce a positive or negative outcome with the public. The most innocuous change can cause a firestorm of controversy if not handled properly. To prevent your organization from experiencing online backlash similar to what Carnival and the Cruise Line International Association experienced, be sure to prepare for both a positive and a negative response by members and customers in reaction to a new concept.

In any given situation, especially if it is a new idea, there is a temptation to think that everyone will love the concept as much as you and your board do. Executives and members get excited; you and your association staff get excited because you are thrilled to actually be moving things forward. The momentum of change is so great that you forget (or choose to ignore) the possibility of a negative outcome. This decision-making style is something that Stephen Forssell, doctor of psychology at George Washington University, calls *the availability bias* (personal communication).

The Availability Bias

The availability bias is the tendency to rely on easily available memories to make judgments. Typically this goes wrong when we use available memories to make judgments about probabilities. Many people, for instance, guess that you are more likely to be killed or injured in a plane crash than in a car accident. In reality the opposite is true. However, because plane crashes are vivid and highly available memories with lots of disturbing imagery, we can mistakenly judge a plane wreck to be more likely than a car wreck.

The same goes for positive events. People tend to overestimate their odds of winning the lottery, in large part due to photos or footage of elated people smiling and holding oversized checks for huge amounts of money. In the case of the association rebranding, which we review in chapter 18 about a viral spiral, the association's board hired a world-renowned branding firm and expected the work to be hailed as marketing genius because that image was stuck in their heads throughout the rebranding process. But the entire membership didn't see it the same way.

Consider how the 24/7 news cycle and social media actually strengthen the availability bias. We remember recent experiences or reports; the news has a significant effect our decisions. For example, images of a cruise ship lying belly-up off the coast of Italy will make people far less likely to book a cruise, even if, statistically speaking, cruises are very safe. Consumers have thus been *primed* by the news and images, increasing the *accessibility* of this information. The association mentioned above was not primed with the information in advance.

Availability biases can result in poor decision making because the decision is based on single, potentially skewed, examples. Understanding how the brain works is important not only to be able to craft campaigns that support the way people think, but also to avoid the biases in our own brains as we make decisions and to think more objectively. Again referring to the unfortunate story of the association that changed its logo/brand and unveiled it at a national meeting, the board's preconceived notion of the branding firm's greatness made them and the staff less likely to criticize the work and think objectively regarding the potential of a negative outcome. In fact, it was a very negative outcome and required massive damage control.

Before your organization makes a big announcement or decision, it is essential that you prepare for and consider the worst- and best-case scenarios. Although not everything will spark a controversy, there are certain topics that are more likely than others to trigger an emotional reaction. Mainstream news topics like veterans, family planning, animal welfare, or fundamental rights get people talking and taking sides. A few fundamental things that garner an emotional response for brands include name changes, logo variations, positioning strategies, a new executive, legislative or customer-facing policy changes, and procedural changes. If you're concerned that a decision or change will cause a SPIKE, good or bad, for your audience, do the necessary research and preparation before making a public statement. If you're anticipating negative feedback, consider investing in focus groups or surveys to gauge consumer or member reactions ahead of time. Also remember the type of members or customers with whom you are dealing. Are they holistic thinkers or analytic thinkers? Believe it not, that will impact how they react to certain announcements and changes.

How Thinking Styles Influence the Blame Game

Negative publicity can affect the way consumers feel about a brand, and it can influence their spending habits. Just ask Lululemon, Chick-fil-A, or Carnival Cruise Line. However, not everyone responds to negative publicity in the same way. A study published in the *Journal of Consumer Psychology* revealed that consumers react differently to negative publicity depending on what type of thinking pattern they exhibit.

According to the journal, people's reactions to negative publicity about a brand are heavily influenced by *attribution*, or where they place blame. When people stop to consider the circumstances, they are more likely to place blame on outside sources as opposed to internal factors.

- *Analytic thinkers* tend to ignore contextual factors, and assign causality or blame to the individual. They're more likely to be affected by negative publicity.

- *Holistic thinkers* are more open to considering all the circumstances, and they are less affected by negative publicity because they consider other factors at play (Monga and John 2007).

Thinking styles don't just apply to negative publicity. They are also directly related to the way consumers view a brand and evaluate their experience. If analytic thinkers have a negative experience with your brand, they'll be quicker to blame the company. Holistic thinkers are more likely to chalk up a negative experience to external factors.

An easy way to understand thinking styles is to examine the way people approach bad service in a restaurant. The **analytic thinker** would immediately label the restaurant as having bad service. A **holistic thinker** would consider the factors affecting the service: Was the server's section extremely busy? Was the kitchen backed up? Was he or she just having a bad day?

Consider the impact this research has on your communications strategy. Tactics designed to influence consumers' *thinking styles* could give you a strategic advantage. If consumers are encouraged to pay attention to contextual factors, like industry problems or third-party suppliers, they'll be less likely to assign blame solely to a brand and less likely to form attitudes based on negative publicity.

Principles of Influence

Regardless of thinking styles, according to Robert B. Cialdini, author of *Influence* (2007), there are six principles of influence that will sway the public:

- Authority
- Reciprocity
- Scarcity
- Commitment and consistency
- Social proof
- Liking

I would argue that there is a lost principle in Cialdini's mix as a result of the changing media landscape. First let's explore examples of the six basic principles and how they can affect your ability to test and determine public response.

Principle 1: Authority

Cialdini uses the idea of influence and how these psychological values are rooted in how we have evolved as human beings. Whether it is to buy a product or joining a membership organization, Cialdini's principles ring true. Let's take the idea of authority. With authority, we feel a sense of duty or obligation to people in positions of authority. As Dr. Forssell explains it, "It is natural for us to respond to authority because as we were evolving as a species, we congregated in small social groups and if you were to challenge the alpha male in your tribe, you were ostracized and left to die." For organizations, using authority is an excellent way to demonstrate that you are the go-to source for content, information, and membership. The "I, too, Am Harvard" photo campaign is a perfect use of the influence principle of authority. The 63 African American students who participated in the online awareness campaign wanted to demonstrate the diverse experiences that black students have at Harvard. The students used Harvard's clout to draw attention to the initiative that directly took on stereotypes of black students and Ivy League campus life. The #itooamharvard campaign was powerful, poignant, and sharable.

The website, hosted on Tumblr, said: "Our voices often go unheard on this campus, our experiences are devalued, our presence is questioned. This project is our way of speaking back, of claiming this campus, of standing up to say: We are here."

Kimiko Matsuda-Lawrence and other members of the Kuumba Singers of Harvard College, Harvard's oldest existing black organization, came up with the idea for the campaign around spring break 2014. The photographs depicted black students holding boards with micro-aggressions and racist remarks they have heard on campus.

You may not have Harvard-level recognition or prestige, but what type of authority does your organization have that you can use to your advantage? Is it research, relationships, recognition, networking, certifications, education, services, staff? What do people turn to with respect to (and out of respect for) your organization? Rank where your organization places compared to competitors.

The American Library Association (ALA) is a great example of an association that is an authority on research and reference services, in the traditional sense. True, the world of printed books has changed as we and libraries know it, but there was no reason for the ALA to abandon its position of authority when it comes to the reason people have typically used libraries. And they didn't. In fact, when it comes to research and reference, many public libraries have used their reputation and the web to move people toward virtual reference. According to a study of public libraries conducted in late 2013, "Virtual reference is embraced in one way or another by the majority of larger libraries and some smaller libraries" (Wanucha and Hofschire 2013, 18). The study went on to show that e-mail, chat, and text reference services are widely used now by libraries everywhere (with text reference services growing the most). "The results suggest that social media, text reference, and mobile access will continue to grow," the report says (35). Additionally, nearly 75 percent of academic libraries supported virtual reference service, according to data from the National Center for Education Statistics (US Department of Education 2011, 16), including e-mail reference (72.9 percent), chat reference (26.6 percent), and text messaging (24.3 percent).

The ALA is well respected, and it successfully used that authoritative position to keep moving forward and to sway its audience toward virtual reference, to advance its own mission online, and to provide even more services. The ALA now provides the best experience for online users by understanding the users' need for mobile accessibility and matching evolving options to technology preferences and information-seeking behaviors.

Principle 2: Reciprocity

It is almost impossible for you not to feel compelled to give back after someone does something helpful. In a study titled "Sweetening the Till: The Use of Candy to Increase Restaurant Tipping," subjects found that if waiters or waitresses gave patrons a chocolate mint, their tips went up 19 percent, compared to patrons who received no chocolates. Further, the study showed that when the server gave the customer two mints and told them they were only supposed to provide one, their tips skyrocketed by 22 percent. A possible explanation for this candy effect is that customers feel obligated to reciprocate the server's generosity by being generous with respect to their tip. Think about how you can go out of your way for your members or customers, which will make them feel obligated to reciprocate your generosity. Perhaps offer a free upgrade to an event, VIP seating at a speaking engagement, or an exclusive opportunity to meet up with a high-profile member they have always wanted to meet.

Principle 3: Scarcity

Georgetown Cupcake, a famous cupcakery based in Washington, DC, had just opened its doors when they hired my firm to generate some buzz. We positioned the up-and-coming shop as a place to hang out while lining up for a tasty treat and turned them into a household name. We used the negative of the long line for cupcakes into a positive event and pitched that to the media as part of the Georgetown Cupcake experience. When cupcakes sold out, we positioned it as scarcity at work. This principle made people want to line up even more. What a great example of scarcity at work. To this day, people still line up for these tasty treats.

Principle 4: Commitment and Consistency

Have you ever encountered someone with a clipboard from an environmental organization asking you to donate to stop abuse of animals? If and when they get you to donate to a cause, the organization has got you hooked. Every time they come to you for a donation and a specific reason behind why they need the money, you will be compelled to comply because you don't want to do something that is inconsistent with your beliefs. You've already committed once, and you want to stick with it.

We all have a strong desire to be consistent, but the trouble is that it can be crippling from a marketing and PR standpoint. Studies show that people making a bet at a race track exhibit a strange uptick in confidence once they commit to betting on one horse over another. Regardless of the odds, once they put the money down, their confidence soars. If you don't think you are guilty of that blind arrogance, consider my personal story:

I was on the phone with a client of mine who works in the winter sports industry and said he had been charging people to renew their contract every summer for the past 10 years, even though his seasonal business provides optimum value during the winter months. When I challenged him on timing, he said, "We surveyed customers and they said timing wasn't something they cared about and we didn't want the renewal date to change." He further explained that they had a 66 percent renewal rate on the first ask, so there really was no need to change the timing. My client wanted to remain consistent, despite the fact that changing the renewal timing could see a huge uptick in renewals. The customers had no reason to tell the association they wanted a change, because there wasn't a significant enough benefit to them. From the marketer's perspective, 66 percent is good enough. Most people choose to avoid the risk of changing and stay committed and consistent with their beliefs even if they are flawed. Carefully consider the beliefs you cherish and why they may be wrong. (Sacred cows, anyone?)

Principle 5: Social Proof

It is human nature to try to figure out the best course of action. One of the best ways to do this effectively is to get opinions from others. This is one of the reasons Yelp (founded in 2004) has been so well-received. In case you're unfamiliar, but I doubt you are, Yelp is a multinational corporation headquartered in San Francisco, California, that operates an "online urban guide" and business review site. According to a Nielsen survey, many Yelp users go to Yelp before making a purchase, with four out of five users saying they visit the site before spending money. As of the first quarter of 2013 Yelp had a monthly average of 102 million unique visitors. You don't need much more social proof than that.

Principle 6: Liking

Ellen DeGeneres is likeable—plain and simple. She is a well-respected brand, hailed by millions of Americans as one of the highest-rated talk show hosts on TV, according to Nielsen Ratings. Samsung used her likeability factor to bring more attention to their new mobile phone. As the main sponsor of the Academy

Figure 12.1.   Ellen DeGeneres Oscar Selfie

Awards, Samsung incorporated their phones into the host's, Ellen's, routine. A simple selfie was planned in advance. What Samsung didn't know was that several other A-listers would jump into the photo. At the 86th Academy Awards Oscars in 2014, Ellen DeGeneres not only snapped a picture of herself, but she asked Meryl Streep to join in the selfie, and other attendees—Jared Leto, Jennifer Lawrence, Channing Tatum, Julia Roberts, Bradley Cooper, Kevin Spacey, Brad Pitt, Angelina Jolie, and Lupita Nyong'o—posed as well. This caused Twitter to briefly crash due to overwhelming numbers of users re-tweeting the now famous selfie. In the first 24 hours, the tweet "scored 32.8 million impressions," according to Mashable (see figure 12.1).

According to *USA Today,* "more than 2.5 million people tweeted the selfie. In fact, DeGeneres' pic has become the most retweeted post ever, more than tripling the previous record holder for most retweets, President Obama's 2012 'four more years' reelection photo" (Barker 2014). This is a terrific example of using the liking principle in marketing.

The Lost Principle of Influence—Friendship

In my opinion Cialdini is missing one critical principle of influence that is relevant in today's social world—the **principle of friendship**. While this is an extension of the reciprocity principle, the friendship principle focuses more on the emotional give-and-take between people. I believe this applies both online and off, and Dr. Forssell agrees. Just imagine this. You are having a conversation with a new acquaintance and he talks only about himself. He never asks you any questions, not one. This violates the friendship principle.

What's implied in conversation banter is the give-and-take and intimacy; the idea is "I listen to you, and you in turn listen to me." It is an unspoken pact between friends and acquaintances. If you are respectful and thoughtful and ask the person in the conversation about himself or herself, there is great benefit to both people. You need to validate the other person's time, as well as your own.

If brands are trying to build relationships with their audiences, fans, and followers through content marketing that is all about the brand and the brand's needs, there is no relationship. It is as one-sided as it gets. However, if a brand demonstrates a commitment to only send information that is important to its audience, the brand demonstrates a commitment to valuing its audience's time, and consumers and members alike are more likely to stay loyal to the brand.

Create a Contrarian Brand Platform to Stand Out

"To a contrarian like me, constant advice not to do something almost always starts me quickly down the risky, unpopular path."
—MICHAEL BLOOMBERG

Managing negative brand perception is equally important as understanding positive perceptions. In fact, the negative perceptions or polarizing facts about your brand, mission, or cause can actually be a powerful way to come up with a creative campaign that penetrates the market. If we ignore these factors, we run the risk of a competitor using our own perceived weakness against us in a marketing or PR campaign.

The cold hard truth is not everyone will like you or your brand and you don't need them to. Margaret Thatcher once said, "If you just set out to be liked, you would be prepared to compromise on anything at any time and you would achieve nothing" ("Interview for Press Association..." 1989). The secret is to get out in front of an issue. Anticipate what others will say about you and admit your brand's flaw(s) with a level of transparency and light humor. Still, they may not like you, but they will respect you ... or at least write a book and produce a movie about you.

Take Anna Wintour, publisher of *Vogue* magazine, who has never been known to shy away from controversy. In fact, many people feel she has embraced her critics and ridden their vitriol to the top. Her steely, demanding, and cutthroat nature was legendary in fashion. It is widely believed that Wintour was the source of inspiration for Lauren Weisberger's novel *The Devil Wears Prada* (released as a film in 2006, for which Meryl Streep won an Academy Award playing Miranda Priestly). Weisberger wrote the novel after an 11-month stint as Anna Wintour's assistant at American *Vogue*. Streep's severe, cold, and ruthless portrayal of Priestly immediately drew comparisons with Wintour and the fashion magazine industry at large. Amidst the media buzz, Wintour could have rejected the rumored stories about her, but instead she embraced the negativity, even appearing at the New York movie premiere dressed in what else but … Prada.

Wintour embodies the Vogue brand and the fashion industry that is known for its exclusion. Streep's Wintour-esque *Devil Wears Prada* character practices and preaches the power of exclusion during a popular scene where Andy Sachs (played by Anne Hathaway) is standing nearby taking notes while Miranda Priestly makes styling decisions for a magazine photo shoot. As an assistant presents Priestly with two belt options and notes how different they are, Sachs sniggers because she thinks the belts look exactly the same and can't appreciate the significance. Priestly then turns on Sachs and targets her oversized blue cable sweater as she begins to explain how it came to be on Sachs's back. Priestly tells Sachs that her sweater is not just blue; rather, it is cerulean and Priestly notes the beginning of that color's significance back to a 2002 Oscar de la Renta runway show. Tracing the color as it trickled down through the fashion filter, Priestly says to Sachs in a condescending and all-knowing tone, "That blue represents millions of dollars and countless jobs and it's sort of comical how you think that you've made a choice that exempts you from the fashion industry when, in fact, you're wearing the sweater that was selected for you by the people in this room from a pile of stuff." Clearly, Priestly is not concerned with people liking her; she makes her point, however, with flair.

Moving on to a well-known brand: Kraft Miracle Whip. The company's campaign of 2013 was cited in a *Harvard Business Review* article. Kraft posed a question to celebrities who either loved or hated the product in a commercial by asking, "What do you think of Miracle Whip?" Celebrities like Pauly D from *Jersey Shore* and the political pundit James Carville gave strong and not so flattering opinions of the sweet mayonnaise spread. The campaign worked, producing a 14 percent uptick in sales, according to the Miracle Whip brand director Sara Braun (Luo, Wiles, and Raithel 2013).

Figure Out What Is Polarizing

How do you find out what the most important things are for your fans, members, and customers? Simple: find the most polarizing people or beliefs in your industry or profession. Think about why those people or ideas elicit such strong opinions. Polarizers are those people in your industry or profession who can divide a room. What they talk about is often what a member or customer is truly concerned with but may not voice themselves. Polarizers reveal extreme views, fears, and opportunities.

Begin with how people rate your product, service, or organization. As a professional speaker, one of the measures of my success is polarizing feedback. It may sound a bit crazy, but when people have either loved me or hated me, I know I've hit an emotional nerve. When I have a bunch of amazing reviews stating things such as, "She is the best speaker at the conference," but in the same batch of attendee evaluations I see, "I don't agree with her at all," I count it as a victory. Brand managers need to think the same way.

Create a Brand-Hater Audit

In the practical sense, brand managers should contact dissenters and ask them why they feel negatively toward the organization, brand, or mission. A brand-hater audit should consist of:

- Honest feedback from the dissenter.
- Careful listening by the brand manager/company to learn about the opportunities for improvement or positioning.
- No defensiveness, blame, or guilt.

If you can't or don't want to do the audit, consider hiring a third-party consultant. Use the information from the audit to build a case with your executives or board to vie for additional resources to address specific organizational weaknesses. Stress the importance of addressing these issues to the executive staff and demonstrate how it will negatively affect the bottom line if it is not fixed.

Anticipate Brand Contempt and Get Ahead of Issues

If you can anticipate what will cause people to react negatively and get ahead of their concerns in statements, communications, or new product announcements, you can save your organization a lot of time worrying about the polarizing issues. You can use the emotional triggers of consumers or members to your advantage.

To pick out a contrarian strategy, focus on issues that are closely tied to your brand—good and, especially, bad. Be sure to acknowledge the internal white lies people tell about your organization and address them by referencing the haters. Trust me, it will help your internal popularity if you are the one unveiling the underbelly of the organization's issues.

For instance, my firm conducted an in-depth message analysis for an association that couldn't figure out why members were so unhappy with the level of service, annual meeting, and programming. After talking with several staff and members, we realized it was the way the organization's employees talked about serious and confidential issues about the event with members. The association's staff used words to describe the association like "chaotic," "three-ring-circus," and "completely overwhelming." With a little tweaking and providing the association with phone transcriptions of our conversations with members, we were able to change the conversation from the inside out by bringing the issue to light. Many times, organizations are the last to admit deficiencies. Letting customers or members speak to them directly can be a way to address them before they become a bigger battle.

Playing Chicken with Your Positioning Strategy

The truth is that when you take a position, not everyone will like it and that is okay. Actually, it means you are resonating with your audience. Some marketing experts recommend "poking brand haters" or intentionally antagonizing brand detractors to create buzz or reinforce a brand's connection with supporters. I believe that is a flawed technique and just plain bad advice. Brand detractors get some level of satisfaction from being dissatisfied. Why give them a bigger forum? Many believe brand advocates will step up to the plate to defend brands they love, but that is taking a chance for very little possible payoff. I have seen well-respected brands in a crisis get very little support from their customers and members as an issue arises. People want to see how you handle it before they get behind the brand. As the old saying goes, don't win the battle but lose the war. Remember that as soon as brand sentiments change, that victory, however short-lived, may come back to haunt you. Consider Chick-fil-A.

Fast-food chain Chick-fil-A came out publicly against gay marriage in June 2012. In a statement, Chick-fil-A's president Dan Cathy said, "Well, guilty as charged," when the *Baptist Press* asked about the company's support of families led only by a man and a woman (Blume 2012).

"We are very much supportive of the family—the biblical definition of the family unit," Cathy said. "We are a family-owned business, a family-led business, and we are married to our first wives."

After a lot of criticism, Cathy softened his tone a bit by assuring his customers that Chick-fil-A will "continue its tradition ... of treating every person with honor, dignity and respect—regardless of their belief, race, creed, sexual orientation or gender" ("Chick-fil-A Exec Takes Stance against Same-sex Marriage" 2012).

But Cathy did not apologize or change his views. In an article published in the *Atlanta Journal-Constitution*, Cathy said, "I think the time of truths and principles are captured and codified in God's word and I'm just personally committed to that. I know others feel very different from that and I respect their opinion and I hope that they would be respectful of mine. . . . I think that's a political debate that's going to rage on. And the wiser thing for us [Chick-fil-A] to do is to stay focused on customer service" (Stafford 2014).

From a brand standpoint, picking issues that are emotionally charged and evocative can drive customers away, but many patrons actually flocked to the fast-food chain in support. According to Chick-fil-A, 2011 sales were $4.1 billion, a 13.08 percent increase over 2010's figures, and same-store sales increased 7 percent.

While the company's position on gay marriage might be applauded by those who share Dan Cathy's point of view in the short term, it is sure to drive many others away in the long run. And if the political debate and laws change in favor of gay marriage, as I suspect they will, companies like Chick-fil-A will be left looking out of touch, old-fashioned, and, at worst, discriminatory. Chick-fil-A will suffer and this will be a mark on their brand for some time to come.

From a PR perspective, when an executive, public figure, or spokesperson like Dan Cathy takes such a stance on a hot-button political issue, the only course of action for the organization that wants to change its position is to pick another spokesperson or distance itself completely from the comments. Unless you can live with a polarizing positioning strategy for the rest of your brand's existence, think twice. The danger in this type of political approach is that consumers may see the bold position to take a stand as a plea for attention and it may backfire.

Dan Snyder: Touchdown or Fan Foul?

Often, brands are forced into a contrarian point of view because a group or following of people have decided to rally against it. Without having made any significant missteps in the public eye, brands can be dragged into the spotlight and forced to comply "or else."

For example, Washington Redskins owner Dan Snyder has repeatedly faced public outcries against the offensive nature of the football team's name and mascot. The football club's 81-year history and widespread following of fans are being challenged by the idea of political correctness and a recent demand for change.

A segment of the public has denounced the Washington football team's name and is working through the government to force Snyder to retire the "Redskins" moniker and adopt something that's more universally pleasing. The problem, however, is that pleasing everyone is impossible. There is more value to a brand than just a name. Truth is, the Redskins fans have something to talk about, even as the team was on an all-time losing streak. Even as the controversy grows, diehard Redskins fans remain loyal and are standing behind Snyder's decision. Fans actually created a Facebook page that says, "Love the Redskins, Hate Dan Snyder," which demonstrates brand loyalty, despite Snyder's polarizing position. The same holds true for business. If you are going to take an unpopular stance like Snyder, you have to marry the position or divorce it completely. You have to be ready to be hated, in order for the brand to be adored. Being somewhere in the middle creates a lack of brand respect and demonstrates weak leadership that will cave under a little pressure; it's like being on the fence. Pick a side and stand there, ready to take whatever comes your way.

Returning to Bloomberg's quote at the start of this chapter, there are clear advantages to being a contrarian: in the investment world from which Bloomberg hails, in the sports arena featuring Dan Snyder, and in the land of marketing and PR, which is where you and I come in. Bloomberg says, "The contrarian instinctively reacts against anything that becomes conventional wisdom." In other words, by looking at things in a way differently, yes, sometimes even opposite, from everyone else, you can find opportunities for your company, cause, or creation.

Checklist for Creating a Contrarian Brand

Make a list of the norms for your industry, product, or profession. See which of the norms you disagree with and use that as a basis. Build out the list and use the contrarian position in messaging, marketing materials, and speeches so you stand out. For instance, many firms in PR respond to RFPs. One of my most widely read articles was why I was giving up RFPs. The title of the contrarian piece: "Why Your New Agency Is Lying to You." Shortly after the piece was published, I secured a year-long deal with a nonprofit who was "sick of the PR firm status quo and appreciated [my] candor."

Say something counterintuitive, so people pay attention. This principle is something we learned in school with "what doesn't fit?" exercises. We all can easily identify with standard practices, but it's what is different that we remember. When you are in meetings, see what you say that hits a nerve for certain people. That usually signifies a strong opinion and is ripe for contrarian opportunities.

Scan the news and social channels. Check out what the influencers are saying. Do you believe there's more to the story? Comment and create pitches, ideas, and stories based on what you disagree with. This will help you find your most contrarian points of view.

The reason that many people tend to take the same side on an issue is that, no surprise, there's safety in numbers. Take a chance on a contrarian point of view and create a SPIKE for your organization.

DANGER SIGN: A word of caution to the agitators: before beginning your contrarian campaign, anticipate and prepare for disagreement from the outset. Prepare a list of potential Q&As, comments, responses, and rebuttal points.

The Fairness Fallacy and How to Call a Time-Out When Things Go Bad

"Life is never fair, and perhaps it is a good thing for most of us that it is not."
—OSCAR WILDE

All organizations, no matter how truly noble their cause, eventually find themselves under attack. Yet there persists a common misconception that good deeds alone will safeguard an organization from scrutiny. We refer to this delusion as *the fairness fallacy*.

What's worse is that decision makers with this false assumption often fail to develop a comprehensive crisis communications plan. Doing so seems like a waste of time and resources because they believe their code of conduct shields them from crises in the first place. Some managers even seem to believe that the very act of developing a crisis plan implies some hidden wrongdoing. And why prepare for what may never happen?

Additionally, this assumption often prevents organizations from developing effective messaging in response to a potential crisis. Rather than addressing the actual cause of the criticism, apologizing, and clearly stating how they plan to rectify the situation, they tend to focus on unrelated positive aspects of their organization.

By far the biggest concern with this belief is that usually it leaves organizations unprepared for or unable to effectively respond in times of crisis. They spend more time discussing the fairness of their predicament than actually fixing it.

I've seen groups of executives go over the fairness of a crisis for literally hours and hours. The typical range is anywhere from four hours to nine and a half hours, belaboring how unfairly they are portrayed by the media, members, and staff.

One client approached us when a well-respected broadcast media outlet that also had a huge online presence was beating down their door for an investigative interview. The client had no plan, no idea what to say, and they were completely unprepared for the situation they found themselves in. But above all, they just didn't think it was fair and it paralyzed them when time was a limited resource.

Our client was fixated on the unfairness, and we heard:

- We've been doing things right for the past 25 years. Doesn't that count for anything?
- The media is just going to take what we say and turn it into a sound bite that will be taken out of context. It is not even worth responding.
- We know the story is already written. Our comments won't influence the piece.
- The media always portrays our industry as the bad guys—why bother?
- Our competitor will probably have already been interviewed for the piece and said all that we would say anyway.
- Even if the media does interview us, we couldn't explain our side with enough depth. The existing consumer bias is too big to take on with one interview.
- No one reads/sees/respects the opinions of journalists at this outlet; why should we give them any credibility with a response?
- We aren't ready to respond—the media needs to wait for when we are ready to tell the full and accurate story.
- They will vilify us no matter what we do.
- We should just say, "No comment."
- Who reads the *Washington Post* and the *New York Times* or watches *CNN* anyway? This will blow over in no time.
- We're above this story. We don't need to defend ourselves.

What a complete waste of time, resources, and effort for any organization. The organization would have done better to strategize how to respond, deciding what information they could bring to the table and which experts could support their case publically.

The truth is that the potential for even the most ethical organizations to experience a crisis does not, in any way, detract from the value of their good deeds. Previous philanthropy and social responsibility can certainly be important aspects of effective crisis messaging; however, they do not negate the crucial need to directly address the cause of the crisis.

Organizations are allowed to make mistakes; they can even make *big* mistakes and still remain in high standing with the public and media. It all depends on how quickly and how well they respond.

Fight or Flight Mode

When we get a call from a client undergoing a crisis, we know from experience that they will immediately go into *fight or flight mode*. And there's a biological answer for why. The body activates the sympathetic nervous system when faced with a stressful event or immediate danger, which triggers people to adopt either one of two modes: get defensive (fight), or bury their heads in the sand (flight). It's a biological response that's hard-wired into the more primitive part of our brain. Be aware of this natural urge and, while calmer heads prevail, make sure you and other staff members are all on the same page about how to respond.

As you face a crisis, understand that decisions and strategies will be made with heightened emotions, and people will say things that are out of character. Take that into account with whatever you are suggesting, and be sure that you do not attack someone's perspective or opinion. Although it may seem like a waste of time, I always suggest meeting with each person on your executive management team individually to build consensus for how to proceed. Doing so slows down the process, but it also provides time for the fight or flight mode to subside. Trust me; it's easier to talk to a calm executive than a scared caveman or cavewoman.

Preparing for a Crisis: Trust Always Trumps Likeability

Communications and marketing professionals are people pleasers by nature. However, concerns over being well-liked oftentimes can have a negative impact on your organization's crisis readiness. Being well-liked is great, but being a trusted advisor is better (PR Epicenter 2012).

If you're concerned about underlying issues in your organization that could create a communications crisis but have been challenged by leadership in the past to address and fix concerns without coming across as the "bad guy," read on (PR Epicenter 2012).

It's essential to keep in mind what really matters to executives when making your case for crisis preparation. It often requires having a few difficult conversations (like bringing up past mistakes or skeletons in the closet or pointing out flaws). But having those difficult conversations before—as opposed to during—a crisis will position you to win, not lose (PR Epicenter 2012). Besides, if you do bring it up during a crisis, your audience is likely to "kill the messenger." In my experience no one wants to hear what they did wrong as it is happening.

Case in point, an executive I worked with once refused to apologize during a crisis that was being covered by 100 outlets online and off because, he said, "I am not the person responsible, and I am not going to take the blame for my employees' incompetence." My response without missing a beat was, "As the CEO of your organization, the buck stops with you." Regardless of how "unfair" he felt apologizing was, it was the thing he had to do as a leader to protect his company.

Stop the Clock

When times are tough, it is easy to get overwhelmed and inadvertently convey a sense of chaos. Calling a time-out is sometimes necessary to ensure the information you are providing is as accurate as it is timely. It requires a statement in the form of asking media (online and off) for the courtesy of more time to ensure that they get the information they need. However, if you're hoping to call a time-out, you must be willing to also offer specific times when the information will be available. For example:

"In light of the recent events, our team requests a brief opportunity to gather the appropriate information. We will have more to share by [date/time]."

This request does two things:

- It allows your audiences to know that you acknowledge the issue at hand and are working to resolve it.
- It gives you until that time to develop additional information, build internal consensus on a response strategy, and prove your desire to remain transparent.

It is critical to stick to whatever time frame you provide. If you do, that could be what people report as so-called progress. Remember, while you build a response, you should continue to have your staff or team monitoring online chatter, blogs, and social media channels. Update and release information on all channels, so it is visible.

Many experts say never to remove a post, comment, or negative feed. I say, "There are no absolutes when dealing with human behavior, especially when they are emotionally charged." Sometimes posts, comments, and feeds warrant removal. This is where crisis experts can be of service. You have to understand what is worth taking down and what isn't. Each move has a consequence, but what matters is how you handle or manage those consequences for your organization.

Develop a Strategy That Works

Keep these key things in mind when calling a time-out and make sure you create a strategy that works (Epic PR Group Staff 2012b):

Identify the real perception issue. Take the time to analyze what the issue is, what audiences you need to be in most constant contact with, what level of involvement your organization needs to have, the needs of your audiences, the degree of seriousness, and so on. These will help your team to craft a more targeted and appropriate apology. Better yet, have a plan in place for issues that may arise in your industry before you need one.

Choose a method of communication. Will you apologize on social media, through traditional media, or perhaps with a posting on your corporate newsroom or blog? Will you use a video statement or a print statement? Whichever platform your organization chooses to use, you must consider your audience—keeping in mind that the more serious the crisis, the more involved the media will want to be. Think about the various factors and the best way to reach the audiences with both the biggest need and the most attachment.

Consult legal. With every issue, there may be legal implications. Thus, before issuing an apology, consult legal to see what you can and cannot say. This will help to prevent a larger issue from developing and will protect your organization down the line. But it's simply not an option to stay silent. Legal counsel prefers to say less, if not nothing at all. The response needs to be a smart strategy from both the legal and PR perspectives. Honest conversations need to be had on both sides.

Get everyone at the table. In any crisis, make sure you have the right people at the table. Consider all the different facets of an issue when creating your "war room." A good war room should have at least the C-Suite, spokespeople, legal, communications staff, and experts in the issue area. Each of these different entities can help an organization craft an apology that is suitable for an audience and that meets their needs.

Avoid Costly Mistakes

After you've developed your strategy, be sure to avoid these costly mistakes communications executives make when executing their strategy:

Defending the brand without a plan. When Greg Smith, a former executive director of Goldman Sachs, made a very public exit, the company seemed stunned. It quickly responded to Smith's *New York Times* article with its own op-ed piece in the *Financial Times*. Interestingly enough they had no plan of action beyond the op-ed and no way to truly address the allegations brought up by Smith. This positioned Goldman Sachs as the giant in a classic David-and-Goliath battle in the media.

Not seeing the silver lining in a crisis. Not every crisis has to be completely negative. Crisis can be an opportunity for change, and oftentimes organizations forget that. The press will pick up on a company's efforts to make a real change post-crisis; whether conducting an audit or reexamining policies, a movement toward change can help ease consumers' worry of the future.

Not picking the right spokesperson. Believe it or not, the CEO is not always the best spokesperson for a company. It is important that he or she remain available for comment during a crisis, but it is not always the best idea to have the CEO as the headlining act. A spokesperson should have superior speaking skills, credibility, charisma, experience working with the media, talking points, and a genuine interest in what is going on. This will help enhance the human element of an issue and make it easier for people to connect with the brand.

Not understanding how competitors will leverage the crisis. When Susan G. Komen announced that they were defunding breast cancer screening at Planned Parenthood, a slew of competing breast cancer awareness organizations began highlighting the work that they were doing. People began to back the underdog. The media picked up on this break from Komen and began writing on the good work and help that these other organizations offered to breast cancer patients and their families.

Not knowing all sides of the story. The quickest way to get into hot water with the media is to comment before knowing all sides of the story. This is where your "war room" comes in. Get everyone at the table to evaluate the situation. Determine the effect of a crisis on different audiences. Decide on a plan of action. This creates a better crisis management strategy. It's better to take time and be ahead now than to speak too soon and have to fall back (or fall flat) in the future.

Positioning the Gravity of the Negative SPIKE

Here are a few quick tips for communicating with higher-ups about getting prepared that won't position you as difficult, negative, or judgmental (PR Epicenter 2012):

- **Appreciate that being a trusted advisor is more important than being liked.** Pushing executives out of their comfort zone to discuss negative issues may make you unpopular at first, but it will help you come out on top in the end.

- **Avoid the blame game.** Provide recommendations and implement strategies … but don't pass judgment as the issue unfolds. That is a surefire way not to get asked back to the table when the next crisis erupts.

- **Provide constructive criticism but never in front of others.** Have those conversations privately to avoid bruising any egos and to keep trust intact. Remember, the executive or leadership team feels responsible without you rubbing salt in the open wound. If you want to provide feedback or advice, do it privately.

- **Understand and respect requests for confidentiality.** Nothing will diminish trust faster than if it gets back to executive staff that you shared confidential details with others. This is so important. Don't speak to your cube mate, best friend, or spouse. You never know who they know or how an issue might come up out of context. Keep it confidential.

- **Consider the "legacy effect."** CEOs, executive directors, and board members want to be remembered for positive changes and smooth operations (not a flurry of negative media articles, blog posts, or comments). Use this concern to make your case for proactive strategies and dealing with the issue as it unfolds, not later.

- **Show them the money.** What does it cost to ignore a crisis? Demonstrate the potential impact, but don't preach. For instance, if a competitor recently suffered a damaging crisis, use that to show executives how damaging a crisis can really become. Also, consider the long-term effects to the brand, reputation, and profits to demonstrate importance. These numbers need to be available before you need them, so get them today.

- **Speak up and be human.** When you provide a compassionate response, you're showing that you can relate to your stakeholders and that you're empathetic. When a crisis unravels quickly, it's tempting to stay silent until you know all the facts and you have a specific update to share. Make sure you provide a response quickly, even if you don't have specific information to provide. It shows you're listening, and you care about what's being said.

- **Provide worst-case scenarios.** Although these scenarios are best done before a crisis arises, they always help people realize and understand how something will potentially unfold when it goes unanswered. Create a quick outline of how a competitor might respond, how social media may be affected, and how traditional media would report on your organization. In my experience, seeing the story unfold gets people back in the moment and helps them work through real strategies instead of focusing on what's unfair, wrong, or missing in the current organization portrayal.

- **Notify and instruct internal staff.** This is a critical area of vulnerability for an organization during a crisis. The leadership team is so busy trying to put out the fire, they forget to tell their staff how and when to respond and to whom. We once had a client whose own staff was quoted as a source in a scandalous piece about the organization's poor management of customers. The employee was trying to explain why the organization was going through problems, yet wound up bad-mouthing systems, practices, and the board. The intentions were good, but with no training in investigative interviews, the employee did more harm than good.

- **Learn from mistakes.** Be sure to debrief with key executives and stakeholders as soon as the dust settles. Offer training, best practices, and lessons learned to avoid repeating the egregious errors. Go through drills on a biannual basis to make sure new leadership is aware of your crisis process.

What's the main takeaway? Whatever you do, provide a solution. If you're going to bring negative issues and concerns to light, come armed with positive, proactive suggestions to be prepared.

Have a Crisis Plan in Place to Handle Negative SPIKEs

"The court of public opinion doesn't wait."
—RONN TOROSSIAN, author of *Immediate Release*

The more than 3.5 billion pieces of content shared each week on Facebook, 234 million websites, and 126 million blogs certainly makes for tricky tracking of online conversations. According to a recent study by Socialcast, 71 percent of social media staff have only one to four years of experience (Horton 2011). This leaves many organizations vulnerable to crisis situations they may not be prepared to handle.

As a first step, we advise clients to create a crisis action team and process for responding. The process begins with fact finding, identifying whether the issue is, in fact, a crisis. Then, assemble the appropriate stakeholders and discuss how to respond or not respond. Answer the following questions to see how prepared you are to handle a viral spiral. This process will allow you to assess your organization's ability to handle a negative SPIKE.

1. Has your organization experienced a crisis online or off in the past?
   a. Yes
   b. No
2. Do you have a process in place to communicate internally and externally with your key stakeholders in the event of a crisis situation?

    a. Yes
    b. No
3. Do you have key messages developed for various crisis situations for key stakeholders and the media?
    a. Yes
    b. No
4. Have you identified the key audiences to communicate with for different crisis situations?
    a. Yes
    b. No
5. Do you have a spokesperson that is poised and well-versed in dealing with the media?
    a. Yes
    b. No
6. Do you have individuals internally and externally that you would consider "brand advocates"?
    a. Yes
    b. No
7. Have you seemingly lost control of social media channels in the past few months?
    a. Yes
    b. No
8. Do you have a "listening strategy" to monitor traditional and social media channels your company is active on?
    a. Yes
    b. No
9. How has your organization responded to negative issues or perception problems in the past?
    a. We ignore PR issues, hoping they'll go away.
    b. We address PR issues, but only internally.
    c. We face the issues head on.
10. My organization is perceived accurately.
    a. Strongly disagree
    b. Somewhat disagree
    c. Neutral
    d. Somewhat agree
    e. Strongly agree

11. How frequently are your spokespeople called by industry trade media to comment/add perspective on issues or trends within your industry?
    a. Never
    b. Rarely (1–4 times per quarter)
    c. Average (1–3 times per month)
    d. On a regular basis (as issues arise media know to call your organization for comment)

12. Do you have at least two executives who are media-trained?
    a. Yes
    b. No

13. How "prepared" do you feel to meet the consumer demand for more transparency?
    a. Very prepared
    b. Prepared
    c. Somewhat prepared
    d. Not prepared

14. Rate how comfortable you are with your organization's ability to respond to a crisis.
    a. Not comfortable
    b. Somewhat comfortable
    c. Very comfortable

15. Are other organizations in your industry currently experiencing a crisis?
    a. Yes
    b. No

16. Do you currently have a crisis management plan?
    a. Yes
    b. No

Scoring System

(1) a. 1, b. 0; (2) a. 1, b. 0; (3) a. 1, b. 0; (4) a. 1, b. 0; (5) a. 1, b. 0; (6) a. 1, b. 0; (7) a. 0, b. 1; (8) a. 1, b. 0; (9) a. 0, b. 1, c. 2; (10) a. 1, b. 2, c. 3, d. 4, e. 5; (11) a. 1, b. 2, c. 3, d. 4; (12) a. 1, b. 0; (13) a. 3, b. 2, c. 1, d. 0; (14) a. 0, b. 1, c. 2; (15) a. 0, b. 1; (16) a. 1, b. 0

0–10 points: You're burning up.

> Should a crisis arise, you're not prepared. Your lack of preparation will result in a slow response or no response at all and your brand will suffer.

11–20 points: You're feeling the heat.

> You're doing some things right, but there is still room for improvement and planning. If you don't take steps to prepare for a crisis situation, you might just find yourself engulfed in flames.

21–30 points: Cool as a cucumber

> Good for you: you've got the experience and the plan to handle a crisis situation and work quickly toward a successful resolution.

16

The Real Benefits of Responding to or Ignoring Negative SPIKEs

"There's no such thing as bad publicity."
—P. T. BARNUM

For years, companies and organizations have relied on the old strategy of burying bad news by putting out an announcement on a Friday afternoon or evening, when people are tired and distracted by their weekend plans. The Susan G. Komen executive team was no different. They thought they could announce their alleged defunding of breast cancer screenings at Planned Parenthood locations throughout the United States without people noticing, simply by releasing the information at 6:13 p.m. EDT on a Friday. Boy, were they wrong.

The fact is, people don't stop paying attention on the weekends anymore. Studies show that social media is actually busiest on the weekends. Posts on Saturdays and Sundays receive 69 percent more interaction than posts on the weekdays (Leibowitz 2012). The ill-timed Susan G. Komen announcement made social media pages light up with protest against the organization. By the following Tuesday, the Associated Press broke the story, and Planned Parenthood was poised and ready with a response (Planned Parenthood 2012). Planned Parenthood's president, Cecile Richards, had received a phone call from Susan G. Komen's president, Elizabeth Thompson, a month prior, notifying her of the coming changes (Associated Press 2012). This gave Planned Parenthood time to develop a strategy and strike at the right time.

As Susan G. Komen muddled through the first week of its unanticipated SPIKE, Planned Parenthood was already taking advantage of the limelight. The Susan G. Komen SPIKE helped Planned Parenthood in several ways:

- Planned Parenthood was handed a perfect opportunity to clear up misconceptions about the organization's role in women's health and highlight mammography as an important service they provide to underserved women.
- Planned Parenthood immediately began speaking out against Susan G. Komen's decision to defund them and solicited donations, online and off. The consumer and media reaction was swift and furious—some would say legendary.

Planned Parenthood sent a fundraising e-mail out to its network, asking supporters to replace the money that Komen had pulled for breast cancer screenings for low-income women:

> I wanted to share some extremely discouraging news from a partner and long-time ally for women's health—news that could have devastating consequences for women.
>
> The Susan G. Komen for the Cure Foundation has announced that it will stop supporting lifesaving breast cancer screening for low-income and underserved women at Planned Parenthood health centers.
>
> It's a deeply disappointing decision—made even more alarming because politically motivated groups and individuals determined to undermine women's access to care appear to have successfully intimidated the Susan G. Komen for the Cure Foundation to withdraw this critical support.
>
> Over the past five years, Komen funds have enabled Planned Parenthood health centers to provide nearly 170,000 clinical breast exams and referrals for more than 6,400 mammograms. These cancer detection and prevention programs saved the lives of women who often had nowhere else to turn for care.
>
> But when anti-choice groups began criticizing the Komen Foundation for partnering with Planned Parenthood, the foundation ended its support for Planned Parenthood health centers. We know our opponents put their ideology over women's health and lives. What we never expected is that an ally like the Komen Foundation would choose to listen to them. (Planned Parenthood 2012)

The e-mail resulted in a windfall of donations and support, national media attention, and a ton of engagement, online and off, for Planned Parenthood. New York Mayor Michael Bloomberg donated $250,000 within 24 hours. All told, more than $3 million came in over four days, and now Planned Parenthood used the money to expand its services and education for breast health (Hensley 2012). They extended the SPIKE by continuing to point back to how the money was raised. Brilliant.

Just three short days after pulling its funding for cancer screenings from Planned Parenthood, Nancy G. Brinker, CEO of Susan G. Komen, apologized for the decision and reversed course. This is where the organization fell short. It would have been better for Komen to stay the course with the defunding, however unpopular the decision was. Instead, Komen released this partial statement (Susan G. Komen 2012):

> "Our only goal for our granting process is to support women and families in the fight against breast cancer," Nancy G. Brinker, founder and CEO of the foundation, said in a statement. "Amending our criteria will ensure that politics has no place in our grant process. We will continue to fund existing grants, including those of Planned Parenthood, and preserve their eligibility to apply for future grants, while maintaining the ability of our affiliates to make funding decisions that meet the needs of their communities. We want to apologize to the American public for recent decisions that cast doubt upon our commitment to our mission of saving women's lives," she said.

Every step of the way, Planned Parenthood used messages and a strong position to create a conversation that was respectful, not opportunistic, as Susan G. Komen fell from grace. After the apology, Planned Parenthood made an official statement, in which President Cecile Richards said, "Planned Parenthood has a 'treasured relationship' with Komen—an organization that has played a significant role in raising the national awareness of breast cancer risk, screening and treatment—and thus, has saved countless lives." Again, this was a smart, strategic, and classy move on Richards's part (Condon 2012).

On the flip side, the controversy hung over Susan G. Komen for years and has negatively impacted the organization's fundraising efforts. As reported by Scott Hensley (2012) from NPR,

"The race in the nation's capital is one of the breast cancer charity's biggest fundraisers each year ... About 25,000 people are expected to take part this weekend, off around a third from last year's 37,000. Races in other cities, including Seattle, Tucson, and Winston-Salem, N.C., have seen similar declines."

Many people will look at this and say it was just a fluke or a lucky break that Planned Parenthood was listening and able to respond that quickly. It is important to note that regardless of how you feel about Planned Parenthood politically, the organization has had its fair share of controversy and unflattering media coverage. That raises the question: Does controversy actually make your organization stronger, more nimble, and better able to respond to opportunities as well as crises? I would argue yes.

When you experience crises often (which Planned Parenthood does because it is dealing with such an emotionally charged, political issue), staff are used to being on both defense and offense for the brand or for the organization's position. Most brands don't elicit this much passion from staff or stakeholders and are more likely to be surprised that a statement or position will get negative backlash. Not Planned Parenthood. The organization knows what hot buttons it can push and how to strategically consider when and when not to take a stand. Do you know what the hot buttons are for your organization? If not, read on.

Managing Negative SPIKEs in Advance

As John F. Kennedy said, "The Chinese use two brush strokes to write the word 'crisis.' One brush stroke stands for danger; the other for opportunity. In a crisis, be aware of the danger—but recognize the opportunity."

A crisis keeps the organization nimble and able to make quick and effective decisions because the toll of not doing so would be too costly and not sustainable. Do you have a good understanding of how clients, members, and stockholders perceive your organization? Have you conducted informal research surveys and interviews to affirm those beliefs? If not, make it a priority to have others articulate their concerns. It will provide you more support and indicate an openness to discussing difficult subjects without getting people defensive. People tend to argue less when they can be part of a consensus than when they see themselves as one lone voice.

Getting departments to own up to perception problems and holes in their strategy is never easy. But the investment in preparedness is definitely worth the peace of mind it will bring you if you have those discussions when calmer heads prevail, rather than in the wake of a crisis or opportunity.

- Do you foresee new issues that may put your organization in a position of vulnerability or opportunity?
- Do people know what to expect because your organization has a strong position on a hot-button issue?
- Have you noticed any increase in negative conversations about industry-related issues coming from your clients or members?
- Do you think there are PR or customer service problems your senior leadership team has tried to smooth over or ignore that may be a crisis in the making?

You should begin to analyze your industry's or organization's biggest issues and rank them according to importance, relevance, and timeliness. External awareness of an issue is an important aspect of this exercise. This can be difficult for associations particularly, because they are too close to their industry or profession to see how others perceive them. Often associations see things through the member-lens. Seeing the big picture can be a challenge and getting members to admit to problems can be an uphill battle. To lessen this insular point of view, one CEO of an association that I know conducts regular focus groups with professionals from a variety of fields. She hires a third-party facilitator, and they report back the findings via transcriptions, key points, and new angles to highlight. Well worth the investment.

Increased Executive Involvement

A good crisis gets the C-suite invested in PR and marketing. Most of the time, leadership pays little attention to the external awareness campaigns and leaves the heavy lifting to the CMO, communications professionals, or marketing staff.

The first place to start in predicting SPIKEs is with past and potential crises. In my experience, across a wide spectrum of industries, a company or individual is never more aware of how, when, and why they are communicating than after a crisis strikes. Do you have an executive team or board in place that can make decisions quickly and effectively, especially under pressure? Rate how comfortable you are with your organization's ability to respond to a crisis. If the score is low, consider using the three P's exercise below with the board, legal and executive staff, and other stakeholders to ensure you have the authority and go-ahead to handle an issue as it arises.

Three P's to Evaluate Importance

Pretend: Imagine that your organization is undergoing a major media and public relations crisis. Picture the issue unfolding with vivid detail. What are the three things you would want to get across? How would you convince others to use your position and ideas to respond to the crisis? Think about this ahead of time and create an action plan before you need one.

Plan: Do you have individuals internally and externally that you would consider "brand advocates"? Think carefully who would be the best internal and external advocates to have on your side. Hold a crisis scenario training with those people in a strategic retreat to ensure you have what you need in place to handle rough waters. Crisis training not only gives staff an education about PR implications related to social media but also gives your business actionable tools to have on hand before a crisis erupts, a crisis which can fluster staff, impair judgment, and cause serious damage to your brand.

Position: Define your organization's positioning strategy related to controversial industry topics. Compile a list of three potential issues or opportunities to comment on that will come up within the next six months. Send out a quick survey to the executive team to get their take, and compile the list for discussion at your next leadership meeting or event.

Had Susan G. Komen given consideration to the three P's before trying to quietly announce a major change in their funding policies, they may have avoided their crisis altogether. They became too insular and too arrogant to realize their potential misstep and wound up paying the price.

Maximize (or Minimize) 15 Minutes (or Days) of Fame or Shame

"In the future, everyone will have fifteen minutes of fame."
—ANDY WARHOL

Long past its 15-minute expiration date, the famous Andy Warhol quote from the 1960s golden age of traditional media still resonates in the age of social media, blogs, YouTube stars, and the Kardashian sisters. But the truth is, Warhol's snappy saying needs to be updated to fit today's "build 'em up, knock 'em down" media-centric society.

After you experience a positive or negative SPIKE in exposure, you have to learn how to navigate the following 15 days of attention that will either bring you fame—or shame. How an organization responds internally and externally in those critical two weeks can make or break careers, companies, and causes.

You may be thinking that in our fast-paced digital world, 15 days seems like an eternity, but we live in a time when the news is covered in more places, albeit with less detail, than ever before. A 140-character mistake can cost a company billions. Our research reveals that the media and public tend to report on and discuss a brand crisis for 15 days or roughly two weeks. Let's take the Public Broadcasting Service (PBS) as an example.

I recently had the distinct pleasure of speaking with Anne Bentley, vice president of communications at PBS. Anne, my former boss at America Online (AOL) and also a mentor, shared how she predicted her organization's SPIKE and capitalized on it.

"As we moved into the presidential election of 2012, we started to hear from Governor Mitt Romney that he wanted to do away with public broadcasting. We were concerned about the ramifications of Romney's statements in the news," Bentley said to me. Her COO challenged her to think about how they could help their local PBS stations make the case for why they should continue to receive funding from a federal appropriation. "He believed, and I agreed, that we needed to quickly and effectively demonstrate how the $445 million dollars from the federal appropriation works. He asked, 'What can we do to help stations push back and make their case?'" Bentley said she gave the response a lot of thought and then sprang into action with a public affairs positioning campaign. "It wasn't easy," she told me. "After thinking about it for a long time and going down a lot of avenues, at the end of the day, we ended up deciding that we would build a site, a digital site, called ValuePBS.org. It was a massive infographic that showed the public why PBS and member stations were of value and essential. We carefully explained why they couldn't do away with PBS. We showed how much we do in communities, how much we do for local stations, and how much we do for parents and kids. And we stressed that the defunding would be a big loss, not just for PBS, but for America," Anne said. This preparation was all before that fateful presidential debate on October 4, 2012.

The first televised debate of the 2012 presidential election took place with Mitt Romney and President Barack Obama sparring off. Bentley sat on her couch at home, waiting on the edge of her seat with the rest of America as she watched, waiting for an opportunity to strike. No one at PBS could have known the precise opportunity that Romney would throw in their laps, but they were prepared to respond quickly and effectively.

Romney said, "I like PBS. I love Big Bird. Actually, I like you, too," Romney said to debate moderator Jim Lehrer, the host of PBS's *NewsHour*. "But I'm not going to keep on spending money on things to borrow money from China to pay for" (CNN Political Unit 2012).

Bentley and her team recognized the need to activate the digital platform and ValuePBS.org website sooner than they had anticipated. "We started by targeting all of the keywords that were trending including: Big Bird, public television, and PBS," said Bentley. Then, we put out a simple tweet: *Find out how PBS and member stations are both valuable and essential.* "The tweet put us right where the conversation was happening," Anne said.

PBS also wrote a press statement saying:

> Governor Romney does not understand the value the American people place on public broadcasting and the outstanding return on investment the system delivers to our nation. We think it is important to set the record straight and let the facts speak for themselves. Over the course of a year, 91 percent of all U.S. television households tune in to their local PBS station. In fact, our service is watched by 81 percent of all children between the ages of 2–8. Each day, the American public receives an enduring and daily return on investment that is heard, seen, read and experienced in public media broadcasts, apps, podcasts and online—all for the cost of about $1.35 per person per year. (PBS 2012)

The immediate results of this SPIKE were incredible. The pbs.org/about site where the press statement was posted received more than 270,000 page views in the days following the debate. PBS saw a 6.8 percent click-through rate (4 times the standard) for the "trusted, valued and essential" promoted tweet that we posted the morning after the debate. In the next two weeks, more than 930 articles were published, resulting in 650 million impressions over the few days following the debate. The CEO of PBS and Big Bird did a satellite media tour and were featured on CNN, CNBC, and MSNBC. People also shared their love for PBS through op-eds, on social media, and through letters to the editor. The outpouring of support for PBS was amazing.

"It was really about taking advantage of the moment," Bentley said to me. "What could've been a total PR disaster for us turned into an opportunity, because the groundswell was enormous." And because they were prepared to act immediately.

What can you learn from this golden eight-foot national treasure about a SPIKE? Be prepared. Anne Bentley came out swinging for PBS and so should you for your organization.

SPIKE-Spotter Takeaways from PBS

Timing and nimbleness is critical for taking advantage of your 15 days of fame. What if PBS didn't respond or responded a week later? The opportunity to lead the conversation would have been lost.

Anticipate why people love or hate your brand. These factors need to be top of mind for any organization as you build an argument in a SPIKE. Be transparent, focused, and deliberate about your positioning. Bentley said that PBS and her team decided to not go after specific politicians or the Republican Party in their response strategy. PBS focused on where they had the authority to weigh in. This is where many organizations stray; stick to what you can defend and support.

Give people and media the tools to advocate for you and your brand. Infographics, memes, "Save Big Bird" photos, op-eds, and a strong digital presence—PBS advocates and the media had what they needed to make the story stay alive in the hearts and minds of the American public.

Be on the right channels. For instance, Bentley and her team used Twitter, traditional media, and a website to create awareness quickly and effectively.

Ride the 15 days of fame. Hundreds of op-eds were then written over the next couple of weeks by people. Charles Blow (2012), in the *New York Times*, talked about how important PBS and public television have been to people's lives and how it's an incredible treasure we all should be proud of.

"I think he thought we were an easier target than we were," said Bentley. "Romney wasn't counting on our nimble, flexible PR capabilities, but then I don't think he knew that so many people would come out in support of us from both sides of the aisle." Bentley and her team at PBS were also hailed as "marketing geniuses" in trade publications and won several industry awards.

Handling the brand shame. Brands that manage a SPIKE crisis well can cut negative coverage time in half, but brands that let the crisis manage them can drag out an issue for several news cycles before the media is done tearing them apart. What used to be a temporary and private screw-up can become public fodder for ridicule or validation, not just for 15 short minutes, but for 15 long, stressful days.

Up and Down the Celebrity Shame Game

Celebrities are often victims of this vicious "shame game." How their publicists handle these issues can be career makers or breakers for their clients. Although Tinsel Town indiscretions may seem worlds apart from everyday business SPIKEs, they are not that different for a company or an association brand manager. The only difference is they are handling the shame on a more prominent stage with more aggressive players looking to damage the celebrities' public personas. Cue Beyoncé and "Elevator Gate."

On May 11, 2014, Beyoncé Knowles, Jay-Z, and Solange Knowles were in for a major brand SPIKE after TMZ purchased and leaked video footage of Solange allegedly kicking Jay-Z in a hotel elevator in New York City after the Metropolitan Museum of Art's Met Gala (France and Balinsky 2014). The press ate it up. Until that time, Beyoncé had a pretty tight hold on her persona in traditional and social media, but this video was the stuff paparazzi dream of. The famous couple was in for a wild ride or, in SPIKE terminology, what we call a "viral spiral." (Chapter 19 is devoted to this entire topic.) A viral spiral is when a video, comment, or issue takes on a life of its own and the public joins in the media spin, creating storylines, plot twists, and feeding the rumor mill with wild speculations to keep the story trending. And, boy, did this story trend. For one whole day, the Twitter hashtag #What-JayZSaidToSolange caught the attention of the whole world. How did the dynamic husband-and-wife duo handle this controversy? Surprisingly well. Let's review what happened. From cheating to lying, the public came up with all their own theories. The next day, Beyoncé posted four sweet pictures of herself and her sister on her account, and Solange followed suit (Davis 2014). Next, Beyoncé's team released a vague but effective press statement via the Associated Press three days after the incident that read:

> As a result of the public release of the elevator security footage from Monday, May 5th, there has been a great deal of speculation about what triggered the unfortunate incident. But the most important thing is that our family has worked through it.
>
> Jay and Solange each assume their share of responsibility for what has occurred. They both acknowledge their role in this private matter that has played out in the public. They both have apologized to each other and we have moved forward as a united family.
>
> The reports of Solange being intoxicated or displaying erratic behavior throughout that evening are simply false. At the end of the day families have problems and we're no different. We love each other and above all we are family. We've put this behind us and hope everyone else will do the same. (Fekadu 2014)

The next night, *Saturday Night Live* did a spoof on the real reason for the elevator brawl: a spider (Ramisetti 2014). Again, a viral video, but then the press began to tune out and Queen B's Elevator Gate came to a screeching halt.

Don't Get Caught with Your "Brand Pants" Down

What happens when you don't hire a team of Hollywood fixers? Let's examine the now infamous interview in November 2013 with Lululemon Athletica founder, Chip Wilson. Wilson said something he would soon regret, when he blamed the company's recent fabric debacle and subsequent recall of see-through yoga pants on the strangeness of women's bodies. "Quite frankly, some women's bodies just actually don't work," he explained to Trish Regan. "It's about the rubbing through the thighs."

Naturally, this classic type of PR misstep was followed by an apology in which a teary-eyed Wilson asked women everywhere to forgive him. He said, "I'm sad. I'm really sad. I'm sad for the repercussions of my actions" (Strachan 2013). Wilson certainly didn't win back any fans with his bizarre apology that basically stated, "I'm sorry that sticking my foot in my mouth has really hurt my company, reputation and my wallet" (Rubin and Dowell 2013).

When that apology backfired, Wilson released yet another video. The second one was even worse than the first. Needless to say, two videos and one mea culpa later his thinly veiled plea for forgiveness made little impact for the now stumbling brand. Chip was definitely in the downward-facing doghouse.

Sales also were impacted by Lululemon's negative SPIKE. After seeing a significant drop in sales, nearly 10 percent after the PR gaffe, the company admitted that comments by its founder and recently departed chairman, Chip Wilson, were affecting retail traffic.

According to a post-earnings call in early 2013 and the *Wall Street Journal* in December 2013, Lululemon's chief financial officer John Currie revealed that the company was seeing a "slowdown in traffic to our stores" (Rubin and Dowell 2013). He went on to say, "I think anytime there is negative PR for our company, there is an impact on the business. I'm not saying we can see a one-to-one correlation, but let's face it. We've had lots of PR issues this year ... And there is undoubtedly some impact on traffic and therefore on the business."

So what could Lululemon have done to manage this shame SPIKE? Wilson and his PR advisors should have let a qualified female executive from the company do the rest of the talking—maybe even a plus-sized woman. After all, Wilson had a history of making controversial comments. In 2004, he said that he named the company Lululemon because the letter "L" isn't part of the Japanese vocabulary and "it's funny to watch them try to say it," the *Washington Times* reported (Chumley 2013).

True, some SPIKEs are unpredictable. However, when you know from experience that you have a CEO who is a loose cannon like Wilson, the company should have been better prepared. If your spokesperson or CEO has a history of inappropriateness, be sure to make a case for intensive media training and suggest a backup spokesperson. Wilson resigned after the media firestorm, but the company is still trying to recover from a sales slump.

What to Do in a Negative SPIKE

The reason most organizations don't address a crisis is because they aren't prepared. They freeze. They simply haven't stopped to consider the most pressing issues they may face. With a little bit of planning, some collective imagination, and crisis scenario training, you can get your organization prepared if a bad spike should hit.

- Begin by thinking about your vulnerabilities. Ask executives to get completely open and honest with you on issues they have dealt with in the past, although this can be a challenge. I can tell you from direct experience that as a crisis hits and executives are thrown into the media lion's den, they become incredibly honest.
- Don't wait. Have the tough meeting before you need to. Rank industry issues and trends that could have a negative backlash. Include crisis basics such as disgruntled employees and major layoffs. If you can begin the conversation with a basic business

crisis, the C-suite tends to pay more attention. Use these types of scenarios to get what you need in place before something else hits.

At the very least, your executives will have some crisis practice and you will have the foundation for support to handle your 15 days of shame quickly. I do recommend contacting a crisis communications firm to get you through the initial media firestorm.

18

Why Wait? Anticipate Negative SPIKEs

"Out of a crisis comes clarity."
—RANDOLPH O'TOOLE

With the SPIKE plan, you can minimize the shame and maximize the fame. Let the crisis serve you, rather than sabotage you. A perfect example of a mismanaged SPIKE is the 2013 *Carnival Triumph* cruise ship debacle.

How Carnival Cruise Ship Sank Its Reputation

On February 10, 2013, the *Carnival Triumph* suffered an engine room fire 150 miles off the Yucatan Peninsula, knocking out power to the 3,143 guests and 1,086 crew members on board the ship ("Carnival Triumph Cruise Ship Stranded in Gulf of Mexico" 2013). The *Triumph* floundered for four days at sea and left passengers and crew to withstand food shortages and unsanitary living conditions. Passengers stranded aboard the ship had no access to elevators, electricity, air conditioning, running water, or adequate food. With no restrooms, repugnant as it sounds, human waste lay all over the staterooms from overflowing toilets and in bags in hallways.

When passengers demanded answers, the cruise director responded with vague promises and limited information. Rob Bonenfant, a passenger, said via e-mail to a reporter for CNN Travel, "Passengers are now really pissed off. Mood on the ship is getting worse among passengers, captain is giving limited information" (Mungin and Morgenstein 2013). Passengers blogged, tweeted, and posted on Facebook about their experiences aboard the ship, and the narrative of an industry in crisis became a major issue for the public relations professionals and Carnival leadership to mitigate as quickly as possible. Social media and the 24-hour cable news industry pounced on the issue and nicknamed the incident "the poop cruise."

It seems inconceivable that Carnival Cruise Lines didn't think that at some point they would have a cruise ship get stuck at sea. Maybe they had a crisis plan—an outdated plan—that didn't factor in social media and people's ability to report a situation with their smart phones. What did Carnival do wrong in its misguided attempt at damage control? What could the company have done right? Let's break down the media coverage over those critical 15 days.

Fifteen-Day Analysis

Week 1

In the first week of coverage of Carnival's disastrous cruise, mainstream media focused on the developments of the incident: a stranded ship, rescuing passengers, compensating travelers. They interviewed people who were directly involved, including Carnival executives, officials, and staff as well as passengers booked on upcoming sailings and families waiting ashore while relatives were onboard. Continuous coverage of this story on A-list news outlets included damaging headlines such as

- Carnival Cruise Ship Floats in Gulf of Mexico after Engine Fire, Will Be Towed—CNN Headline News
- Carnival's Reputation Springs a Leak—NBC News

Though the cruise ship limped to port, the coverage continued and took on quite a severe and judgmental edge: "Carnival Cruise Tells Passengers They Can Keep the Bathrobes in Total PR Fiasco," according to a headline from the *Huffington Post*. *Saturday Night Live* even did a skit on how gross the situation was onboard the ship, while mocking Carnival's horrible response.

Carnival, like a lot of companies, may have been able to predict that one of its ships would someday have a mechanical problem, but what the company simply wasn't prepared for were the hundreds of passengers who became embedded reporters while the company handled a customer service debacle.

Before social media, a company could perhaps quietly deal with an issue like this, but not anymore. Now, consumers have the power over the brand message. The only way brands can get ahead of these types of issues and avoid a PR disaster is to have a proactive plan in place to deal with the most common issues, provide the utmost transparency, offer constant updates, and have social media responses ready to go. Seven days may have once been a quick turnaround to respond and deal with breaking news or a hot story, but today a week's time practically equates to ancient history.

Week 2

During the second week of media coverage, traditional media gradually zoned out. Stories were mainly analysis and comments rather than reporting. Interviews were conducted with experts in fields such as crisis communication, law, travel, consumer advocacy, and safety. As the media lost interest, new coverage consisted of mostly trade publication coverage and online news sites with mentions in mainstream outlets: "How Carnival Went from 'Fun Ship' to 'Poop Cruise'" (Business Insider.com) and "Carnival Cruises Tries to Dig Themselves Out of Another PR crisis" (Bulldog Reporter).

The lesson, more so today than ever before, is that news coverage of an incident even of this magnitude subsides after two weeks, but the media were watching Carnival carefully, and consumers were waiting for them to mess up again. What the Carnival brand managers didn't consider was the fact that it was on *PR-obation*. I refer to *PR-obation* as a brief but critical span of 90 days after a crisis, when a company will be highly scrutinized for any misstep, however inane.

Fool Me Once

Any additional slipup after a crisis becomes national news can further erode consumer confidence. And this is precisely what happened to Carnival just a month after events aboard the *Triumph* hit the news. When the *Carnival Dream* was stranded in

St. Maarten a month later, the media, not surprisingly, jumped right on the story. To avoid further embarrassment to the company, Carnival quickly flew its passengers home. But the damage from the *Triumph* incident stuck. The headlines were not kind:

- Carnival Hits More Choppy Waters—CNN
- Carnival's New Debacle—CNBC
- New Carnival Nightmare—Fox News

This time, the novelty wore off faster, and with the passengers safely home, coverage faded out after one week, rather than *Triumph*'s two. However, the combination of the tandem incidents cast a pall on the entire cruise ship industry and led to headlines like this:

- In the Wake of Ugly Incidents at Sea, the Cruise Industry Is in Hot Water—*Time*
- Cruisin' Takes a Bruisin' in the Eye of PR Storm—*USA Today*
- Cruise Ship Sinking: Carnival's Disaster Upsets the Whole Industry—*International Business Times*

What would it have taken to avoid these headlines followed by consumer mistrust and right the ship on a course that would end positively for Carnival?

"Fortune Favors the Bold"

Instead of remembering the ancient Latin proverb and doing something bold to address their issues, Carnival relied on denial and obfuscation. Meanwhile, passengers aboard the *Triumph* used their cell phones to update their families. The families talked to traditional media and vented on social media, sharing horrifying tales of food shortages and dark staterooms awash in human waste. By not getting bravely in front of their problem, Carnival essentially put the media and the public in control of spinning their story. They permanently damaged their brand and made their entire industry look suspect.

When a crisis strikes, it is often difficult for leaders to take the wheel for a variety of reasons. But all too often, executives and their respective PR teams get caught up in putting out one fire after another, without considering big-picture brand consequences.

In order to gain consumer trust back, Carnival executives would have had to fundamentally change the way they did business. What if

- The company had taken all of its cruise ships off the ocean for a dedicated amount of time to show consumers they were serious about fixing mechanical, structural, or other maintenance issues?
- Carnival had made an announcement about what they were doing to remedy the issues to ensure they didn't happen again?
- Carnival hadn't continued with "business as usual," hoping this embarrassing incident would blow over?

No matter how well a damage-control campaign is executed, actions speak louder than words, and this is never truer than when a company fails to deliver on its brand promise.

100 Days Can Be an Awfully Long Time

One of the most puzzling things about the way this cruise line PR debacle was handled was how slow and unprepared the cruise industry was to react and provide comment. The industry responded *100 days* after the incident with an action plan to protect consumers called a Passenger Bill of Rights. Needless to say, they didn't get much press attention for their very tardy response to an issue that made national and international news for two straight weeks.

It is hard to believe that the Cruise Line International Association (CLIA) didn't think that one day it would have to communicate about a broken-down ship from a member carrier, but that is the reality of what happened in this situation. Considering umpteen legal teams, CLIA board members, and Carnival itself debating what should be included in the Passenger Bill of Rights, 100 days may actually be a pretty quick turnaround time, but it is not quick enough to shape consumer perceptions about taking a cruise. Having the structure, resources, and team to react to such an industry-threatening incident should be a top priority for any organization.

Figure 18.1.   The Carnival Cruise Line SPIKE.   *Source:* Courtesy of Epic PR Group

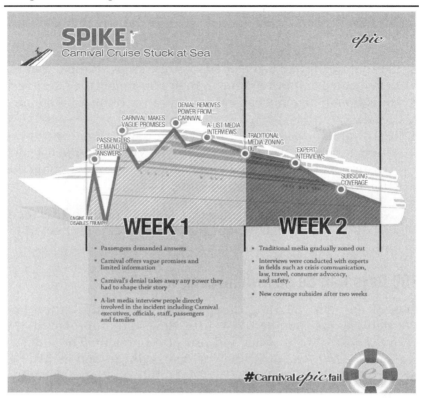

Think about how long it would take your company, organization, or industry to respond to a similar incident or, really, any crisis that affects member perception or consumer loyalty to the brand. If you think it is 100 days or more, keep reading (see figure 18.1).

Here's the good news: organizations not only can predict SPIKEs, they can get ahead of them and turn them into **brand opportunities for themselves and, potentially, major stakeholders**. In other words, they can turn the ship around quickly and successfully, rather than watch it sink while hopelessly standing by with no life preserver.

Anticipation Checklist

- Understand and anticipate the most common negative things that can happen to your organization, members, profession, or industry.
  - Keep an eye out for developing issues or opportunities. If you are the cruise industry, a ship caught at sea, as well as passenger travel issues, should be on your list.
- When the stakes are highest, do you have a dedicated team member who is equipped to listen carefully and respond to consumer or member issues online in real time?
  - Make sure the person has all the passwords and permissions before an issue or opportunity occurs.
- What is this team member listening for during the crisis?
  - Make sure the person is looking for positive and negative commentary, blog posts, traditional news articles, e-mail lists, online and off. And, once the person comes back with the information, get a mid- to senior-level person involved to determine a LPA (Listening Plan of Action).
- Do you have Google Alerts set up with positive and negative phrases attached to your brand, executives, event titles, speakers, and key campaigns?
  - Create Google Alerts that have negative search terms such as *stinks* and *bad customer service*.
- Do you have content that can be easily adopted or changed based on common crises issues?
  - Create a list of potential responses for a variety of channels and platforms based on common crises your industry faces.

The point is to listen and anticipate potential issues. We all will make mistakes. The quicker you can respond to a negative SPIKE, the more respect you will receive from the public. The longer you take and the less transparent you are, the more quickly trust erodes.

Don't Spin Out of Control, Manage the Viral Spiral

"When you face a crisis, you know who your friends are."
—MAGIC JOHNSON

When it comes to handling a viral spiral, a SPIKE that has gotten out of control, organizations need to make sure they prepare ahead of time. This will save headaches, panic, and money down the road. A viral spiral is when a customer service issue, idea, or announcement creates a brand mutiny. These types of viral spiral SPIKEs happen more now than ever before because your audience has more power and influence over your brand's voice. While not impossible to control or predict, these online incidents are serious and must be addressed quickly to avoid long-term reputational harm.

A perfect illustration of a viral spiral is in the following story. One of our clients decided to change the name of its association with very little input from its members. The brand change was actually done in secret and the organization had members who knew about the exciting announcement sign a nondisclosure agreement. They didn't want anyone to steal the thunder of the brand's unveiling. The board unanimously voted in favor of the name change and was so confident in the new brand, they decided to announce it in a very public forum—at the national conference.

Unfortunately, and predictably, the name change was met with some serious resistance, which may actually be putting it too mildly. The association's members took to social media and for a solid seven days complained about the organization, its leadership, and the lack of opportunities for members to be involved. People were upset, vocal, and frustrated. Everyone had an opinion.

Right after the conference, one frustrated member turned to social media and rallied her followers to protest the name because it came a little too close to her own materials. Although she had very little proof of a trademark infringement, the public supported her outcries and sided with the perceived underdog. The association's hands were tied—they were caught up in a viral spiral that was spinning out of control.

Announcing Change

How could the association have prevented this from happening? What follows are techniques for announcing change, something many people have a lot of trouble dealing with.

1. **Prepare a soft launch.** The *Chronicle of Philanthropy* describes a *soft launch* as something that is "generally used when a business doesn't want to draw a great deal of attention to a product right away; they want to gradually introduce the new product or changes to the market." When announcing something that will be potentially met with resistance, test the market in order to avoid a PR or marketing disaster (Strait 2014).
   - Write a few short blog posts talking about the possible need for change and how it could affect the organization, to gauge people's reaction.
   - Call a few members or customers at random and ask them for their feedback on the possibility of a change.
   - Based on the initial reactions of members or customers, you can help your staff anticipate positive and negative comments.

   The bottom line is that a soft launch is less nerve-wracking, costs less to implement, and gives you and your employees time to get better prepared for questions, online and off.

Examples of soft launches are found everywhere in the computer and technology world and the rationale shouldn't be lost on associations. Angry Birds, the game sensation developed by Rovio Entertainment, for example, soft-launched earlier this year a new game in the series, called Angry Birds Stella (Nelson 2014). It was shown only in Canada, Australia, and New Zealand in order to test a smaller population's reaction, tweak product inadequacies, and garner opinions before it launches worldwide (Nelson 2014).

2. **Know your critics.** With any announcement, be sure to gather your most vocal and critical members and customers. Often, gathering the most polarizing opinions (as mentioned in an earlier chapter) can help you prepare for the best and worst possible outcome of the change.

   The shoe brand TOMS listens to critics so well, in fact, they've used it as a differentiation strategy. The premise of TOMS is every time you buy a pair of shoes, the organization gives a new pair of shoes to a child in poverty. Some have argued that TOMS has failed to alleviate poverty because shoemakers aren't getting the wages they deserve from the company. However, TOMS founder Blake Mycoskie addressed the criticism head on and said, "The criticism—whether it's true or not—is a fair one, and if you're building a brand you have to listen to the critics, and we have. So, yes, this is addressing not that specific comment but more the comment of 'aid is not enough.' That criticism is a very fair one, because if you build a company to the size of TOMS that's able to do real good and create jobs then why not do it?" (Parmar 2013).

   What a smart response! It probably wasn't done by chance. It was a carefully crafted media message. He addressed the critics, understood it was a problem, and squashed the negativity with an announcement that positively reflects on the brand (Parmar 2013).

   What can you learn from TOMS? Deal with the implications and come out with a public solution and address the critics' biggest concerns. You'll gain brand loyalty and build brand equity that you may want to, or at some point need to, cash in.

3. **Form an advisory council.** Membership organizations as well as corporations need to keep member and customer needs and opinions in mind when making a big announcement. Therefore, give them a structured forum to share their concerns, such as an advisory council. Set the group up like a focus group. Ask poignant and real, nonleading, questions. Record the feedback and share member or customer concerns with your board to provide third-party support for the possible reactions—good and bad. Have others help build your case for preparation.

   Many associations have completed this exercise successfully when they have launched a new magazine, e-book, or educational product. Get the right people together beforehand to react to a new concept, topic, theme, or aesthetic feature; record input; then act on results.

4. **Establish rules and expectations.** If you don't have rules on your social media pages, put down this book and make it a top priority. When things go bad, and they will at some point, you want to provide specific member or customer guidelines to avoid the online Dr. Jekyll/Mr. Hyde personalities from appearing when people are upset.

   Here is an example of social media House Rules on Facebook from Coca-Cola for consumers: "This is your Fan Page and we encourage you to leave comments, photos, and videos here. However, we will review all comments and will remove any that are inappropriate, offensive, or contain external links. We will leave what you share that relates to the subjects covered on this Page. Please understand that comments posted to this Page do not represent the opinions of The Coca-Cola Company." Coca-Cola goes on to explain specific terms of use including what specifically the brand will tolerate. If you set the tone, your members and customers will respect your position and ability to delete, remove, or regulate your brand's channel (Coca-Cola 2014).

5. **Gather brand supporters (*before* you need them).** In an effort to cultivate more positive dialogue with members or customers through traditional as well as social media, pick up 10 positive

brand ambassadors to vet. Have staff reach out to these folks to "take their temperature" on their willingness to contribute positively to the organization's online conversation.

Every conversation will be different, so empower brand advocates to respond to their peers. If they are amiable, share positive tweets, Facebook posts, LinkedIn responses, and Instagram photos. In our experience, people react better to peer-to-peer communication than when the organization tries to control the conversation directly. Have these people ready to provide peer-to-peer response on your behalf should an issue arise.

6. **Create messages and FAQs to anticipate and address member support or opposition.** Do this in advance of when it is critical. Create standard language that can be adapted for any issues that arise. Include a list of potential crisis issues that the organization has or will face in the future and employ crisis scenario training, asking people to respond. Always have a variety of groups and people who react on your behalf; otherwise it will seem staged. Test and review the messages people use and edit them for use. Distribute messages to the *crisis response team* (CRT) and adapt them as needed for your viral spiral.

7. **Roll out with board role-play to answer difficult or negative questions.** When rolling out a new brand or a major change for your organization, role-play with your executives and board members so they know what to expect and how to answer difficult questions. Don't forget to hold conference calls with chapter presidents, high-profile volunteers, and your internal staff. Consider doing both in-person and online training with a crisis communications firm to run through crisis scenarios. This will give you a sense of who the best people to pull into a crisis might be.

Handling a Real-Time SPIKE

Create a command central. Gather the appropriate parties, such as legal representatives, executives, human resource staff, crisis communications experts, and decision makers. During the crisis, create a place on your company's website or blog where you can address issues as quickly as possible via a Q&A document. If you can't create a blog or website on short notice, give people a place they can offer feedback offline, such as an e-mail address or dedicated telephone number. Provide appropriate information via the company's Facebook, Twitter, and LinkedIn accounts and provide feedback to show you're listening.

Get legal counsel on the hook. In many instances, response strategies can be stymied because legal counsel is not available or getting back to you or your client in a short time frame. Many times attorneys that don't work in a crisis environment do not realize the sense of urgency. Be sure to set an expectation of a quick and expedited turnaround on legal matters—pay extra if you have to—but make sure they are on the ready. It's that important.

Be as transparent as you can. Why did the Tiger Woods scandal get so much press? Among a few other things, it was because his PR team did not address the issues from the beginning and they left the media to speculate, causing a flurry of misinformation. First and foremost, be transparent about not being able to answer at the time of the crisis and assure your key stakeholders that you will provide more information at a later time. Say something.

Don't let your social media audience rule the conversation. Crisis communications is a time where leadership and a straightforward approach are paramount.

Decide early if you are apologizing or not. Understanding timing has major implications when apologizing too quickly. Always remember: every move you make in a viral spiral has a countermove or a consequence. Apologizing too quickly or reversing a decision can make your organization's leadership and board look weak and ineffective. It may also embolden your online constituents to revolt every time you make a change or decision they don't agree with. If you do apologize, be sure to be sincere and follow through. (Learn more about the Apology Trifecta in chapter 15.)

Determine what conversations warrant a response. Not only must you have a place where consumers can ask questions about their concerns, but your PR team should determine which questions can and will get answered. Look at the negative conversations to see what people are really thinking, then respond accordingly. Develop an online Q&A at a central location on your website to answer consumers' as well as media questions related to the crisis that your company is comfortable answering. Think about how big a customer's or member's reach is and factor that into whether or not to respond. For instance, if a member has 100,000 followers and is complaining, they should be one of the first people to reach out to and calm down. Organize people by their influence.

Use traditional media as a platform. Don't forget that traditional media will tune into your social media presence as soon as a crisis breaks, to get a sense of what others are feeling at the moment. And they can and will use that information in a story. Get back to the basics here. Social media isn't just another tool; it is an extension of your brand's story. Be sure you, rather than the first responder, are the one telling it.

Use video responses to humanize an issue. Video is an excellent way to handle negative conversations. Avoid writing talking points because the executive will look like a corporate robot with long-winded, teleprompted answers and will wind up looking defensive. Short sentences and honest emotion convey that your executive and your company understand the severity of the issue. Apologize, explain what you're doing to correct the crisis, tell the people why it won't happen again, thank them for watching, and shut off the camera.

If things get heated, make a call. Assign a board member or brand advocate to make phone calls if members are getting irate or frustrated in a public forum. It may not be a pleasant conversation, but it's a must to make sure people feel like you are listening to their concerns. Before picking up the phone, make sure your board member or brand advocate has been media-trained and is comfortable handling tough, unscripted questions.

Ego, the E-Ego (and other factors) on social media. Recent psychological research seems to indicate that the Internet has a Dr. Jekyll/Mr. Hyde effect on behavior, alluded to earlier in this chapter. Whether it's obsessively checking e-mail, online bullying, or indulgent shopping sprees, the Internet has spawned new forms of human behavior, according to Ellas Aboujaoude, a psychiatrist at Stanford University (Epic PR Group Staff 2013). The eerie reality of this phenomenon is that negative traits bolstered by online activity are hard to control. Aboujaoude researches the human "E-Ego," which describes how today's Web 2.0 culture bolsters negative character traits, like narcissism, childishness, and grandiosity. These traits seem to take on new meaning in one's digital life (Epic PR Group Staff 2013). A few traits that gain new life online include:

- **Mean-spirited behavior.** Online bullying does not just come from anonymity online. On the Internet, there is no organized hierarchy to answer to and therefore people behave worse than they would in person. Establish "house rules" (like Coca-Cola) to help weed out this type of behavior.
- **Childishness.** A lack of consequences has activated regressive tendencies, Aboujaoude says (Epic PR Group Staff 2013). A disregard for punishment can result in impulsivity and irresponsibility.
- **Self-Aggrandizement.** The Internet is so customizable: we listen to iTunes that only plays music we prefer, and aggregate our news based on our particular preferences. People become used to having their tastes perfectly matched, with minimal effort, which leads to a sense of entitlement, according to Aboujaoude (Epic PR Group Staff 2013).
- **FOMO (Fear of Missing Out).** According to Dr. John M. Grohol on PsychCentral.com, this phenomenon is defined as, well, exactly that. It's the fear of missing out on something that is perceived as being more fun, or of learning that someone else is doing something more exciting, interesting, or better than we are doing it. It's back to the ego. He says that "FOMO is a very real feeling that is starting to permeate through our social relationships" and, I would argue, seep into our customer and member relationships as well (Grohol 2011).

What is the antidote to a runaway "E-Ego"? Self-awareness. Recognition. Recognizing that we tend to let our ideas run wild online helps us curtail less-than-desirable behavior. Identifying our online patterns that leave us feeling bad is the first step to avoiding problems down the road. Given the prevalence of

Internet phenomena like the E-Ego, it's more important than ever to be prepared for a viral spiral. If negative online chatter is damaging your brand reputation on social media, take charge with a crisis response strategy.

To avoid these negative online personality traits from rearing their ugly heads during important organizational changes and announcements, consider implementing a full-scale approach to responding to positive and negative feedback. Expect the best and prepare for the worst.

20

Dark Websites See the Light of Day

"It was the possibility of darkness that made the day seem so bright."
—STEPHEN KING, *Wolves of the Calla*

Although some SPIKEs can be as scary as a Stephen King novel, others allow us to show our organization's fortitude and perspective. It is important to understand that telling the *full story* is not always an option in the media. Therefore, it is necessary to create a channel, microsite, or series of webpages that better explain your point of view. We refer to this compilation of work as a *dark site*. While the term seems ominous on its face, the idea behind it is to offer a simple, effective resource for an organization that is trying to capitalize on a moment or defend a brand.

Ideally a dark site's content should be prepared in advance and be ready to publish quickly to the Internet. The main purpose is to keep various audiences and stakeholders informed and updated as an issue unfolds. What some perceive as a form of spin is actually just good business planning and preparation.

Dark sites will often become the hub for all official communications related to a crisis and the place to which people are referred from social media channels such as Twitter, LinkedIn, and Facebook for more detailed information. The dark site can be a landing page within the organization's current website infrastructure and populated with PR messages, real-time updates, and information specific to media, stakeholders, and consumers. The site should remain "dark," that is, unavailable to the public, until it is appropriate.

Additionally, the way in which the crisis situation unfolds will ultimately determine the type and variety of resources that will be added to the dark site. In any case, you can anticipate the basic questions that consumers, media, and members will want answered.

A Well-Oiled Dark Site

In 2010, BP was responsible for the biggest offshore oil spill in U.S. history. Eleven people died in that disaster, which simultaneously destroyed the livelihoods of families and businesses up and down the coast and negatively impacted area tourism. The media were unwavering in their accounts of the incident and America became fixated on the company's response. BP's CEO Tony Hayward was the spokesman for the company, and his approach to dealing with media questions and interviews was the PR quagmire of the century (so far). The way the company handled the disaster was also terrible: slow, unclear updates, a poorly framed approach to dealing with the spill, and constant lobbying for environmental waivers from federal agencies.

The company should have provided more consistent updates to the media and its stakeholders as well as to the families affected. The company's CEO should have taken responsibility for BP's part in the disaster, but in an interview with ABC's George Stephanopoulos, Tony Hayward said:

> I think we've made enormous strides as a company in the last three or four years with a remorseless focus on safe, reliable operations. Ah, this wasn't our accident. This was a drilling rig operated by another company. It was their people, their systems, their processes. We are responsible not for the accident but we are responsible for the oil, dealing with it and cleaning the situation up. (Champion and McCarthy 2010)

In addition to placing the blame elsewhere, Hayward notoriously declared, "I want my life back," as part of an insensitive apology caught on video that went viral. Many lessons on how not to handle a crisis can be learned from the BP response, but the company's dark website for the relief effort was stellar.

In the end, BP wound up paying $4.5 billion in criminal damages to the U.S. government and $7.8 billion in settlements with individuals and businesses. The company focused on sealing the well to prevent future spills, cleanup operations, and beaches that were being revitalized in the effort. In the dark site, the company included sections on how they were attempting to make the situation right, a response timeline, the response in pictures, and the response effort via videos. Moreover, the dark site included an interactive map, claims section, and supporting resources for site visitors.

Creating a Dark Site

To create a comprehensive dark site for your organization, consider these essential and recommended elements.

Essential Elements

1. **Provide an overview of your dark site's purpose.**
One of the first things to consider is how you will position the dark site. Like anything else in marketing and PR, first consider your audience. Who are you trying to reach? Whose perspective are you trying to change? Write a campaign headline that supports the main goal for information. BP used a "Make It Right" approach to addressing the damage they caused emotionally, environmentally, and economically. Do a quick SWOT (strengths, weaknesses, opportunities, and threats) analysis for your crisis. Focus on the way in which you want to be seen if the best-case scenario should unfold and be empathetic, transparent, and human in stating the goals. Be careful not to overreach your promises, because people will construe that as spin or lying.

2. **Provide contact information.**
Designate a spokesperson or a team as media point persons for all inquiries. In our experience, streamlining the requests to a few select contacts will ensure consistency and maximize responsiveness. To choose a spokesperson, be sure it is someone who appeals to the audience and is contextually the right choice for the incident at hand. For instance, having a British spokesperson for an oil spill that mostly affected the southern United States was not the best choice, because his accent made him seem callous and cold to

the down-to-earth Southerners whose livelihood was destroyed as a result of the oil spill. BP would have been better off using a local spokesperson who could appeal to and understand the impact of the spill on the region's economy and culture.

3. **Offer an interactive timeline (if appropriate).**

To demonstrate how an organization is handling an issue, deliver a timeline with detailed information on what you are doing behind the scenes to get the crisis rectified. With silence, the media, stakeholders, and general public will make their own assumptions and create their own versions of the story. By providing a timeline with updates, you can better control the message and make the company seem transparent. Without information, the organization seems like it is hiding something or, worse, doing nothing to remedy the situation.

4. **Give background on the incident.**

Background information that helps promote clear understanding of the situation (for example, the cause, nature, and likely impact and what is being done to eradicate or deal with the matter at hand) is imperative to being transparent. On the dark site, it helps the audience understand the entire situation.

5. **Provide regular updates.**

Create "skeletal" versions of regular industry updates to facts about the crisis situation and actions being taken. We suggest creating an e-mail subscription opt-in or a Twitter handle, where the public and members of the media can be informed of updates on a regular basis.

In the case of the missing Malaysian Airlines flight MH370, the airline's initial response to the disappearance came out on March 8 at 7:24 a.m., five hours after the loss of contact with the plane, according to an article in *PRWeek* (Tilley 2014).

The *PRWeek* piece further explained that the airline activated a dark site and began giving regular, but sometimes inaccurate, information to the government and the press based on speculation, with the intention of keeping the public at bay. This inaccurate information led to an initial search in the South China Sea where precious time was wasted in finding the missing aircraft. As a result, the airline lost credibility, time, and most importantly, public trust. Having a dark site is important, but providing accurate, credible information is more important. A significant lesson to learn from the Malaysian Airlines PR gaffe is that dark sites are only a tool. They alone don't replace good, transparent corporate or association reporting.

6. **Develop a comprehensive press kit.**
Develop a comprehensive press kit describing the crisis event and response. Sometimes we recommend a video message from the CEO or other board members (when appropriate), but only if they are likeable and camera ready. Be sure to get them media-trained before you need them to go on camera. In our experience, putting a CEO or executive through the wringer allows you to see how well they would do in a mock worst-case-scenario interview as practice under pressure.

We worked with one association CEO who was asked to appear on a well-respected investigative TV news show because her whole industry was under fire for unsafe medical practices. To prepare for the crisis we did a mock interview with a reporter and camera in our studio. During the training, our client came across professorial but condescending. She was visibly uncomfortable, yelled at the media-training reporter, and was fidgety. Her body language made her look guilty and her tone encouraged the reporter to keep asking more questions. Although she was not the best spokesperson, she did the interview anyway because she insisted that if she didn't, the board would fire her. Big mistake.

I tell this story not to paint this CEO in a bad light, but to emphasize that there is an all-or-nothing approach in the midst of a crisis that can be avoided. This type of situation and others like it is the reason you conduct media training prior to a crisis.

Media Training #1: Train a Spokesperson

Plenty of huge company CEOs never see the spotlight (there is a reason for that), and they are perfectly okay with that setup. To make your CEO feel comfortable, be sure that your spokesperson is well trained and has experience garnering positive interviews for your organization in advance of a crisis. Build a case for why the spokesperson is the most experienced, well-rounded person for the job, and provide the CEO with an opportunity to suggest messages or stories for the spokesperson to share so that he or she feels included in the strategy.

Recommended Elements

Industry information. Create general information about the industry (including leadership, history, "Swiss cheese" press releases, FAQs, track record on important subjects, media footage, b-roll). This information can be utilized by association members or members of the media during the heat of the crisis issue.

Media Training #2: Cultivate Advocates

Trying to find advocates in a crisis is like trying to find a needle in a haystack. It is downright difficult, if not next to impossible. Before a crisis strikes, determine which association members and customers could be contacted for additional comment or an industry perspective. Be sure to have these people engaged with your brand in a positive manner before approaching them. Building up a cadre of people who will come to your aid in certain scenarios should be a part of any crisis plan.

Lists. Gather a list of reports and links that are accessible to the public to show your association or company is informed and is a resource for its members, customers, and the media. Be careful not to include information that does not pertain to the situation at hand or seems too self-serving. Offer resources and data people will use to build a case for you, not against you.

Infographics. Create an infographic that visually represents your industry or the situation and any relevant information. A visual is easily understood and shareable across social media networks. And it is much more appealing and more widely read than words on a screen. One of the top infographics in 2013, according to Piktochart.com, is shown in figure 20.1 explaining just why a brain actually craves infographics.

Responsive design apps. A new trend that is sweeping the design community is responsive design apps for a smart phone or tablet. Responsive design is meant to keep people interested and engaged in app content in a way that is seamless. For a crisis situation, this type of an app can be developed to tell a fully interactive story about the crisis, using videos, live links, and ways to connect all the information about the crisis in a less static way.

Figure 20.1. Why Your Brain Craves Infographics. *Source:* Courtesy of Danny Ashton of NeoMam Studios

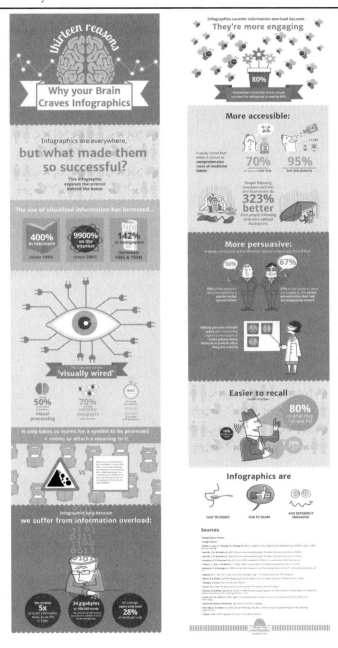

Updates in real time can also be integrated in the app to ensure that people are getting accurate information. The same type of app can be used in a positive SPIKE.

Myths-versus-facts sheet. This tactic ensures the media are reporting accurately on the issue, profession, industry, or company. To make this clear to anyone interested in the story, develop a "myth versus fact" section that debunks industry misconceptions.

Third-party experts. To support the organization's position and add credibility, engage third-party experts (academics, scientists, historians, gerontologists, etc.) and include them in your media outreach strategy, alongside vetted spokespeople.

Repurposed content. Repurpose and edit much of the video and website content that most likely already exists on your website on a related SPIKE. If you have done what I have recommended in previous chapters, you'll have a list of the potential SPIKEs and be able to access this categorized material in advance. This content will serve as additional proof in the value of various audiences.

Password-protected information. Should organization members become increasingly anxious about a crisis, create a tailored section of the website just for them that only they can access. This will show that you are listening and hear their concerns. You should include a crisis assessment, specific resources to consider, and a hotline to contact staff for emergency purposes.

Search engine optimization (SEO) and track-back campaign. Consider a keyword strategy and even SEO campaign to push people to the dark site from search engines (if possible, develop a list of search keywords before a crisis hits).

Whatever information you decide to include, it should always be focused on the essential facts and could consist of a couple of succinct web pages. The design should be clean and simple with the sole focus on offering information. It is vital that this not be seen as a marketing piece.

Evolve the Site as Needs Change

In our experience, an organization's dark site will need to evolve over the course of a crisis or opportunity, however short or long that time frame may be. For example, at first the focus may be on providing people with emergency information, then move to more detailed information related to what is being done to solve the crisis, and finally switch to the aftermath and plans for making sure a similar event never happens again.

A dark site is a first-rate tool to get ahead of and respond to media inquiries and the organization's key stakeholders in real time as the crisis or opportunity unfolds. Be prepared and turn your intentions into actions. As we all know, actions speak far louder than any words ever could.

The Underdog versus Top Dog Effect

How Some Brands Pick Themselves Up and Come Back Stronger

*"Leadership almost always involves thinking and acting
like the underdog. That's because leaders work to change
things, and the people who are winning rarely do."*
—SETH GODIN

There's no denying that everyone loves an underdog. We tune in to the Olympics in record-breaking numbers to hear stories about young athletes and their struggle against the odds. We are inculcated from childhood with the appeal of the underdog—characters like the hobbit Frodo Baggins in *The Lord of the Rings* or a team of misfits in *The Bad News Bears,* and we celebrate "Cinderella story" victories in sports and life. Who hasn't heard the story of J. K. Rowling, billionaire author of the Harry Potter stories, and her humble beginnings as a single parent who barely had enough money to pay for the paper to finish her first manuscript? And what about the character Rocky Balboa, the Italian Stallion, who went from punching meat to cashing in ringside? In both the movie itself as well as in Sylvester Stallone's writing of the manuscript and refusing to allow anyone but himself to play the role, it was the underdog coming out on top. Finding and telling your underdog story is one of the easiest ways to create a SPIKE for you or your organization.

Interestingly, our love of the underdog also applies to the brands that we believe in and influences choices of consumers and members. According to recent research published in the *Journal of Consumer Science* (Paharia, Keinan, Avery, and Schor 2011), an underdog brand biography increases purchase intentions and brand loyalty by consumers. An underdog biography typically comprises humble origins, a lack of resources, and a struggle against the odds. Consumers identify strongly with underdogs; and thus they identify strongly with underdog brands. The study found that, regardless of demographic, respondents considered themselves to be an underdog—even though many were white and living in above average socioeconomic conditions.

The brand biography is an unfolding story, which chronicles the origin of the brand, its struggles, and its evolution over time. The underdog usually exists in relation to an opponent who has abundant resources and is favored to win, aka the "top dog." Prior to this study in the *Journal of Consumer Science*, there hadn't been a lot of research published on the effect of the underdog story on consumer choices.

Sara Blakely Spanx the Hosiery World

A perfect self-made billionaire underdog story is Spanx founder Sara Blakely. She took $5,000 and an idea for footless pantyhose, and turned it into a women's hosiery empire. People love Spanx as a brand, not just because they carry great products, but because Blakely's road to success is so unique. Her success in the male-dominated hosiery industry makes Blakely's the perfect underdog story.

Prior to founding Spanx, Blakely had never taken a business class and had never worked in fashion or retail. In fact, at the time she came up with the idea for Spanx, she was selling fax machines door-to-door. One day, she cut the feet off of a pair of control-top pantyhose and the rest is history. Blakely is now the world's youngest self-made female billionaire. She owns 100 percent of her company, has had no investors, and has yet to spend any money on advertising. So how did she turn Spanx into a globally recognized company that generates over $250 million in annual revenues ("Power Women" 2014)?

She had the drive to succeed, the determination to make a better life for herself, and the persistence to work hard until she did. She created her own prototype, convinced a hosiery mill to produce her product, cold-called Neiman Marcus to make her first sale, and submitted her own patent online after reading a book on how to write one.

In addition, many high-profile people like Jimmy Fallon, Lance Armstrong, and Mark Sanford all position themselves as evolving from humble beginnings. The giant, Apple, and others position their products or services as ideas that made it against all odds. Associations and nonprofits can also use this type of approach to identify with and attract customers, donors, and members through carefully crafted messages and tactics.

Who Doesn't Want to Be BFFs with Jimmy Fallon?

Jimmy Fallon. Good looking, class clown, boy-next-door type who is best friends with Justin Timberlake. What's not to like? There is no question; Jimmy Fallon embodies that special quality that we all strive for. But what is it? How can we define it? Most important, how can we get it? He is a classic underdog. Fallon is the friend we all want. He is kind and witty and sometimes childish. He knows how to sock us in the arm to get us to lighten up. For example, he started off his first episode as host of *The Tonight Show* by saying, "I'll be your host, for now." He referenced his wife, his baby, and his parents at which point he joked that he tried to get them "better seats." He showed appreciation for his band, his long-time friend and announcer, and the audience for tuning in. He went on to say, "I want to do the best I can, and take care of the show for a while, as long as you'll let me." The audience is rooting for him to do well because he seems to be striving for success. Yet, by anyone's standards, he already is successful.

In a hilarious skit, Fallon made a bet with friends for $100 that he would never be the host of *The Tonight Show*. In his true self-effacing form, he had a cadre of stars from Hollywood, including Robert De Niro, Lady Gaga, Sarah Jessica Parker, Joan Rivers, and Lindsay Lohan each give him $100, proving they were all wrong about him. Every brand can learn from the way he approached his *Tonight Show* debut.

Lance Armstrong's Reputational Battle

The Lance Armstrong story of a rise to sports stardom seems like a plot to a Hollywood movie—a classic underdog story. Here is an excerpt from Bio.com about Armstrong's battle with cancer:

> In October 1996, however, came the shocking announcement that Armstrong had been diagnosed with testicular cancer. Well advanced, the tumors had spread to his abdomen, lungs, and lymph nodes. After having a testicle removed, drastically modifying his eating habits, and beginning aggressive chemotherapy, Armstrong was given a 65 to 85 percent chance of survival. When doctors found tumors on his brain, however, his odds of survival dropped to 50–50, and then to 40 percent. Fortunately, a subsequent surgery to remove his brain tumors was declared successful, and after more rounds of chemotherapy, Armstrong was declared cancer-free in February 1997.

After he survived cancer, Armstrong went on to become one of the world's best-known cyclists and many credit him for the growing popularity of the sport in Main Street America. He married a public relations executive, Kristin Richard, and had two children. After his marriage ended in divorce, Armstrong dated Hollywood A-listers such as Sheryl Crow, fashion designer Tory Burch, actress Kate Hudson, and TV star Ashley Olsen. He was living the dream until one day the man who biked 15,225 miles (mostly uphill) to win seven Tour de France titles, appeared to be giving up. But I guess that depends on your definition of giving up. In late 2012, as the US Anti-Doping Agency (USADA) took his coveted titles and banned him from cycling professionally, Armstrong was still earning $78,000 a day from his work with the LiveStrong Foundation, according to *Forbes* (Rishe 2013).

With his skillful positioning as an underdog, Armstrong transcended the topic of performance-enhancing drugs. In the middle of a scandal, the conversation focused on his work as a great philanthropist and dedicated husband and father, qualities that few refute. Essentially, he made himself untouchable. As *Washington Post* veteran sports columnist Sally Jenkins (2012) writes: "Lance Armstrong is a good man. There's nothing that I can learn about him short of murder that would alter my opinion on that."

He made the USADA look like a bully and himself its hapless victim. Even in instances when a person's (or brand's) innocence is in question, the public tends to be very sympathetic and even supportive of those that have been victimized. Like he had any choice?

On August 23, 2012, Armstrong issued an official statement that he would no longer legally fight the USADA's efforts. Armstrong's skillful wording positioned the USADA as an aggressive bully whose sole goal was punishment regardless of guilt. Perhaps more important, he presented himself, his family, his charity, and ultimately cancer patients as victims. Let's examine the wording he uses to describe the USADA and himself in online statements and interviews as his titles were being taken:

USADA: Bully, one-sided, unfair, nonsense, punishing me at all costs, nothing even remotely fair, broken the law, turned its back on its own rules, stiff-armed, threatening everyone, challenging the good faith, at U.S. taxpayers' expense, toll it has taken, in opposition to all the rules, not right.

Armstrong: Family, foundation, truth, good faith, responsibility, devote myself, beautiful kids, fighting cancer, fittest 40-year-old on the planet.

His statement was a non-admission:

"There comes a point in every man's life when he has to say, 'Enough is enough.' For me, that time is now," Armstrong said in an online statement around this time. "I have been dealing with claims that I cheated and had an unfair advantage in winning my seven Tours since 1999. The toll this has taken on my family and my work for our foundation and on me leads me to where I am today—finished with this nonsense."

In an interview shortly after this statement with Oprah Winfrey on OWN, Armstrong admitted to using the hormones cortisone, testosterone, and erythropoietin (also known as EPO), and conducting blood transfusions to boost his oxygen levels:

"I am deeply flawed ... and I'm paying the price for it, and I think that's okay. I deserve this," Lance stated during the interview, adding that he took illegal drugs as a professional athlete due to a "ruthless desire to win ... the level that it went to, for whatever reason, is a flaw."

In October 2012, Armstrong stepped down from LiveStrong, and the way the foundation handled the controversy was textbook crisis management. The major takeaway from Armstrong is to get out in front of a falsehood as quickly as possible and tell the true story before others tell it for you.

Mark Sanford: The Political Comeback Kid

Equally alluring as an underdog story is a great comeback kid, always liked by the American public, which is why some politicians get reelected with a less than perfect past.

Political pundits were in disbelief in 2013. Former GOP governor Mark Sanford defeated Democrat Elizabeth Colbert Busch, the sister of comedian Stephen Colbert, in South Carolina's first congressional district. The governor had made national headlines just a couple of years before when, after having been missing for one week, he admitted to having an affair. The notorious governor even lied about his whereabouts. He was pressured to resign as chairman of the Republican Governors Association and was censured by the state assembly for ethics violations and faced impeachment hearings. In his address to the people of South Carolina, Sanford called himself an "imperfect man" who was "saved by God's grace," according to a *Washington Post* article by Rachel Weiner (2013).

It just goes to show that when you handle the backlash of an issue with a little sobering self-critique, voters will forgive and, in Sanford's case, forget past indiscretions.

Apple's Garage-Made Fortune

Apple was founded in Steve Jobs's garage with Steve Wozniak in 1976 in a modest home located in Silicon Valley. For decades, Jobs competed with Microsoft, finally surpassing Bill Gates and Microsoft in 2010. This was an important part of the company message for years and still resonates with consumers. As Jobs once said, "I'm convinced that about half of what separates successful entrepreneurs from non-successful ones is pure perseverance."

Before positioning your association or company's brand a certain way, contemplate how members see themselves. People like to think of themselves as the underdog, and they identify with underdog stories that remind them of themselves. The results of the study imply that it is wise to position your brand's philosophy as an unfolding story because it increases the likelihood that consumers will identify with the brand and will purchase the product or service.

To demonstrate how much we love the sweet smell of success, the house and garage where Apple was started was named as a historic site in 2013, according to an article in Mashable on October 29, 2013 (Strange 2013).

The Underdog Is You

So what can you and your organization gain from an underdog strategy? People will be rooting for your success, stand up for you even when it may not be warranted, and support you through a personal or organizational crisis. Here's how to pull off positioning yourself as an underdog:

Be humble. Everyone hates someone who brags, so be humble. It will do a world of good for you, your brand, and your customers, especially if you are ever faced with a brand crisis. Understate your accomplishments. It is always better for someone else to recognize your success. A third-party endorsement, whether by media, clients, or stakeholders, is much more convincing than you tooting your own horn.

Be thankful. Thank everyone. Name them. Show appreciation. Hold client retreats, events, and parties. Acknowledge birthdays, anniversaries, and major milestones. Heck, send something to your clients when they least expect it. Additionally, thank your staff publicly; it will make them appreciate and respect you more as a leader. It will go a long way.

Be able to laugh at yourself. When Fallon was debuting on *The Tonight Show,* he knew that some people thought he was too young to take Jay Leno's place. Instead of ignoring that perception issue, he faced it head-on with a joke about a bet. Brands can also do this through strategic messaging. Ignoring an issue won't make it go away, but addressing it could minimize its impact. A perfect example of this is when a social media manager for the American

Red Cross mixed up her personal Twitter with the organization's Twitter and posted the following (awkward) post: "Ryan found two more 4 bottle packs of Dogfish Head's Midas Touch beer … when we drink we do it right."

The Red Cross took a unique approach to handling this flash crisis and posted this humorous response acknowledging the "rogue tweet": "We've deleted the rogue tweet but rest assured the Red Cross is sober and we've confiscated the keys." In this case, the Red Cross was able to minimize damage by quickly addressing the situation, remaining honest and transparent, and even making a joke. Acknowledging the post and keeping an honest, laid-back approach worked well in their favor. And Dogfish Head, the beer mentioned in the tweet, even acknowledged the incident by asking fans to donate to the Red Cross via Twitter.

Be celebratory. Fallon's fun and engaging skits are a great way of celebrating his new late-night post. Similarly, when an opportunity comes your way in business that you can celebrate with others, always remember your audience first. Instead of focusing on the changes or opportunities your organization is facing, think about how those adjustments will affect your clients, staff, and shareholders. This counterintuitive approach will not only help you craft stories and products that resonate—it will help your brand take on a persona more like Jimmy, the friend you always wanted.

The Pedestal Principle

"We like to put people on a pedestal, give them one character trait, and if they step outside of that shrine-like area that we blocked out for them, then we will punish them."
—MADONNA

While the material girl may be the most scrutinized public figure of her day, she is also one of the most talked-about singers in her generation. When she is on the media's pedestal, she stays there for a long time. Be it a controversy or a charitable event, Madonna knows how to play the media and her fans to her advantage. The Wall Street Goliath Goldman Sachs should have learned from this eighties pop sensation that you never get defensive, you get even.

I refer to *the pedestal principle* as brands that are on top and suddenly get knocked off by the media or their own stakeholders. Companies like Goldman Sachs were especially vulnerable after the 2008–2009 recession.

In 2012, on the heels of recovering from one of the worst recessions in U.S. history, largely caused by financial sector mismanagement, Edelman's Trust Barometer released findings that showed consumers were beginning to trust the financial sector a bit more than they did the previous year. Ironically, this announcement by Edelman was made on the same day that Goldman Sachs executive Greg Smith issued a damning resignation letter calling Goldman Sachs "toxic" and "destructive." The op-ed, which appeared in the *New York Times*, was reportedly vetted by the paper's editorial staff before being published. This raises the question: if trust was so high, why did this issue receive so much play?

In the past, e-mails from disgruntled employees went to a limited audience when someone was let go abruptly. Now, the way people share information has made what would otherwise be water-cooler gossip into a public relations nightmare for a major company. Everyone has been in Greg Smith's shoes at one point, but most people didn't have the nerve to write an op-ed in the *New York Times* about it. It is a classic underdog positioning strategy, which we explored in more detail in the last chapter. However, given Smith's affluence, the underdog positioning is a hard pill to swallow. It is basic human nature to want to watch as someone does what we know we couldn't. And this was heralded by the *Huffington Post* as a "dream job exit." Here is an excerpt from Smith's letter:

> I truly believe that this decline in the firm's moral fiber represents the single most serious threat to its long-run survival. It astounds me how little senior management gets a basic truth: If clients don't trust you they will eventually stop doing business with you. It doesn't matter how smart you are.
>
> Without clients you will not make money. In fact, you will not exist. Weed out the morally bankrupt people, no matter how much money they make for the firm. And get the culture right again, so people want to work here for the right reasons. (Smith 2012)

Unfortunately, the way Goldman Sachs responded to this op-ed may be one of the biggest PR missteps of all time.

Get Off the Pedestal or Risk Being Kicked Off

Goldman Sachs commented on Smith's rant, but didn't directly address the accusations or issues. The company's response just fueled the fire. Goldman Sachs's original statement in response to the op-ed:

> We disagree with the views expressed, which we don't think reflect the way we run our business. In our view, we will only be successful if our clients are successful. This fundamental truth lies at the heart of how we conduct ourselves. (Schwartz 2012)

Why did Goldman Sachs seem so defensive? Had they taken the high road and responded with a less defensive tone and a more human approach to the matter, they may have seemed less petty. For example, consider the rewrite suggested below:

Greg Smith has been a valuable employee at Goldman Sachs for the past 12 years and we are saddened to see him take this type of a position in such a public forum. Our culture has been based on providing excellent client service for more than 140 years and we stand by this fundamental truth.

As you can see, the first statement made the company look like they are hiding something, whereas the second, softer statement made Smith look bad. Either way, many will argue that the firm may not have won any popularity contest regardless of its response, but it could have lessened the focus on the firm.

This was a costly PR mistake—a $2.15 billion mistake to be exact, as the stock price took a dive after the controversy. Goldman Sachs missed the opportunity to be seen as an organization under attack by one disgruntled executive. Instead, the firm was stuck defending its position in what became a multiday media firestorm. The company didn't learn from how its first statement was received by the public. Instead, Goldman Sachs responded to Smith's op-ed with a letter to the editor in the *Financial Times*. The second letter was even more damning than the company's original statement, citing an internal study that shows how happy people are about the work they do at the firm.

> ... While I expect you find the words you read today foreign from your own day-to-day experiences, we wanted to remind you what we, as a firm—individually and collectively—think about Goldman Sachs and our client-driven culture.
>
> First, 85 percent of the firm responded to our recent People Survey, which provides the most detailed and comprehensive review to determine how our people feel about Goldman Sachs and the work they do.
>
> And, what do our people think about how we interact with our clients? Across the firm at all levels, 89 percent of you said that that the firm provides exceptional service to them. For the group of nearly 12,000 vice presidents, of which the author of today's commentary was, that number was similarly high.
>
> Anyone who feels otherwise has available to him or her a mechanism for anonymously expressing their concerns. We are not aware that the writer of the opinion piece expressed misgivings through this avenue, however, if an individual expresses issues, we examine them carefully and we will be doing so in this case.

Did Goldman Sachs really expect the American public to believe an internal study? The study seemed like a thinly veiled attempt to show that Smith was wrong. In the past, this type of a PR response may have worked, but not when people can openly discuss the company without retribution. This open dialogue and consumer demand for transparency needs to be factored into any response. What you say will get talked about, but it is up to you as a business owner, company president, or communications pro to predict what people will say and do as a result. The data is out there, as is basic experience dealing with controversy.

Like Goldman Sachs's experience with Greg Smith, external perceptions of an industry have internal implications. At the time the op-ed was submitted by Smith, the financial sector was being crucified for corporate greed related to the mortgage meltdown, and Smith knew that Goldman Sachs was vulnerable. He made his exit strategy and had the perfect opportunity to stage an attack. Goldman Sachs responded defensively and at the wrong time and, consequently, got kicked off the pedestal by the media and public at large.

Questions to ask yourself are:

- How would your executives handle this type of a situation?
- Would they be defensive or operate offensively?
- Would you or your organization get knocked off your pedestal or would you have a strategy to respond and come back stronger?

Most organizations don't have the right processes in place to respond well, but we'll examine one organization that did precisely that and what you can gain from being prepared and aggressive right after a mistake.

Domino's Pizza Gets Attacked and Comes Back Stronger

In 2009, Domino's Pizza had a rough year, after some rogue employees videotaped themselves doing some distasteful things with a cheesesteak and a pizza pan. Within 24 hours, the employees' grotesque video clips were viewed 200,000 times and people were hammering Domino's on a variety of social media channels. Domino's reacted slowly to the online criticism, but once they did react, they shut the store until crews could sanitize the operation and the employees were fired. The original videos, now taken down by YouTube, but still available elsewhere, have been viewed about 2 million times (Evangelista 2009).

Domino's released a video apology (viewed a total of 650,000 times) with the CEO Patrick Doyle; online conversations about the incident also skyrocketed (York 2009). Essentially, they did what they had to, but they also brought more attention to the issue. Traditional media also caught on and started airing parts of the clips, which also caused more interest and searches for the video. Although this could have been a damaging and hurtful fall from the pizza pedestal, what Domino's did next was worthy of a PR-comeback gold star. Domino's saw this as an opportunity SPIKE to drive change and reposition the company for success. The campaign was a perfectly executed act of what I call "disruptive transparency," which spiked not only awareness but revenue as well.

Domino's introduced the Pizza Turnaround Campaign, which showed advertisements that ran on TV with real focus groups ripping the product to shreds, saying that it had a "cardboard crust" and equating the pizza sauce to ketchup. In the ad, Doyle swore to do better and introduce a new version of the pizza. Additionally, Domino's put up a 4,630-square-foot billboard with customer comments that were positive, negative, and indifferent (Wasserman 2011).

Although the campaign "put a knot in my stomach," Doyle said, according to *Adweek,* he did what no other brand had done before or since (Stanley 2010). He poked fun at his own product. According to an article in Mashable, "the campaign was a hit, increasing sales by double-digits in the first quarter it ran" (Wasserman 2011). Since then, Domino's has continued to strive for transparency by vowing to use un-retouched pictures of its pizzas in its ads. And Domino's is once again on the pedestal as one of the top three pizza chains in America.

Paula Deen: Comeback Queen or Fallen Star?

At age 52, Paula Deen had been plagued by panic attacks and for years had barely left her house. In 1989, after she divorced her husband, Paula launched a catering business (on $200 in savings) and eventually broke her phobia. The business was called

The Bag Lady. She and her two sons would deliver sandwiches to local businesses at lunch time, which eventually led to her opening up a restaurant called The Lady and Sons and was widely successful. Next, Paula was pitched for a show on the Food Network and the public fell in love with the Southern version of Martha Stewart and her fried chicken.

In 2012, Paula Deen's brand was beginning to experience some growing pains after she announced that she would be a spokesperson for a diabetes drug called Victoza. The $6 million deal brought Deen some criticism as she had previously positioned herself as the queen of fried food. The deal was launched alongside Deen's announcement that she had type 2 diabetes. The little-known but critical fact here is that Deen had been diagnosed years before with the disease, and yet was still cashing in on the fried food fan-base (Moskin 2012).

The second big hit to Deen came in the form of being accused of uttering a racial slur in a deposition related to a discrimination lawsuit. In the deposition, Deen admitted to using the N-word several times and once wanting black waiters to play slaves in a wedding party she was planning, according to a *Poynter* article (Deggans 2013). Moreover, Deen was invited to appear on *The Today Show* to clear up misperceptions and when she didn't show up, she instead released an apology video that went viral. The video was criticized as being scripted and heavily edited by crisis communications experts in a *USA Today* article (Blas and Clark 2013). *The Today Show* then reported that Deen said, "She was physically unable to make it."

On June 26, 2013, Deen rescheduled her appearance on *The Today Show* for an interview with Matt Lauer. Lauer, known to be a hard-hitting journalist, didn't pull any punches. One question Lauer asked was whether or not Deen was on *The Today Show* to clear up misperceptions or to salvage millions of dollars in sponsorships and partnership dollars. Deen expressed that she was not and wanted to clear up any misperceptions people had about her. Additionally, Lauer pressed Deen and asked, "Given the same circumstances, would you have fired you?" She said no. On the interview, Deen seemed scripted, dramatic, and tearful, yet insincere. Several sponsors and brand partners disassociated themselves from Deen after the botched interview including Walmart, QVC, Caesars Entertainment, diabetes drug company Novo Nordisk, Target, and Home Depot, among others (Shaw 2013).

If I were counseling Deen, I would have encouraged her to admit the wrong, address how she was going to rectify it, and recommend that she not talk about the impact the crisis had on her and her family. The public at large would have shown her more sympathy. Can Paula Deen stage a comeback if she plays her cards right? I think the answer is yes. The major takeaways from these pedestal principle examples are:

- Respond quickly. I recommend responding within two to four hours, but definitely within one day of an incident.
- Don't make excuses for bad behavior.
- Be as transparent as possible regarding the changes to come.
- Explain how you are righting the wrong (even if you still think you are right).
- Invest in a campaign to turn things around.

You certainly don't have to invest $75 million like Domino's, but you do have to make an effort to rectify the misperceptions. The public wants to know you recognize your mistake, own it, and are doing something about it in a public way. It is money well spent. Whether it's a person, company, or association that is plunging from the pedestal, it's all about how they break their fall. Those decisions and actions will dictate whether they are able to climb again or remain on the ground. Just ask Madonna, who's still recording hits and enjoying the limelight—30 years after her song "Holiday" topped the charts.

23

Internal SPIKEs

"Each customer is like a tiny bundle of future cash flow with memory"
—DON PEPPERS AND MARTHA ROGERS,
AUTHORS OF *EXTREME TRUST*

I was recently in Las Vegas for a conference, and I stayed at a hotel on the Strip that the conference organizer booked for me. A bellman, let's call him John, was helping me find my room and set down my bags for me. The hotel lobby was disorganized and as we got on the elevator, the door made a creaking sound that made the bellman cringe. Although he didn't say anything directly to me, I could tell he was a bit apprehensive about showing me to the room. As soon as I entered the hotel room I could tell why. The room smelled like day-old cigarette smoke and looked like a suite that Elvis Presley and the Memphis Mafia may have stayed in in his heyday in 1974. Needless to say, it was poorly maintained and highly trafficked.

Without me uttering a word (my body language must have given away what I thought of the room), John said, "I know. These rooms haven't been updated for a really long time and I'll try to get the front desk to spray for the smoky smell. If you want, I can probably ask to have you transferred to a different hotel. I'm not sure I'd be comfortable having my own daughter stay here."

He went on to explain that the hotel used to be one of the best in town until new management took over and let it all go. He was clearly not an advocate of the changes or current management. I did wind up transferring hotels, per his recommendation, but that got me thinking. How many other people had he stopped from staying at the hotel? How many times had he told other female guests that he wouldn't let his own daughter stay there? What were the financial implications of his actions, attitude, and negative message over time to guests?

The case of a poorly maintained hotel is extreme. However, it should get you thinking. What does your staff say about your organization when you are not there to guide them? Do you have a strategy for the dialogue? Often your employees and internal audience are an afterthought. But they can be your biggest advocates or your loudest critics.

From Starbucks to Comcast, internal communications departments are taking charge of initiatives that connect employees with customers and members to solve problems, answer questions and concerns, engage in conversations, and generally raise the company's profile. For example, Starbucks received 94 out of 100 in *Fortune*'s "Best Companies to Work for in 2013." The Great Place to Work Institute conducted a "trust index survey," one-third of which is based on responses to the workplace culture audit, which includes pay, benefits, internal communications, training, recognition programs, and diversity efforts. The breakdown for the study was 280 firms in 45 countries with more than 246,000 employees.

Employees now affect how your brand is positioned, not just internally, but externally as well. Take a cue from some of the biggest companies in the world investing in employee communications, training, planning, and execution. It could save you thousands, millions, or, in the case of Goldman Sachs, billions.

To organize your employees, consider creating internal personality profiles and success stories, statistics, and shared experiences related to those job duties. This will help differentiate the messaging that is used to talk to someone who is a member or customer or someone who works for your organization on a temporary basis on the trade show floor at the annual conference. The messages and stories that they use to talk about your organization can have a massive impact on brand perceptions and potentially on your bottom line.

To help you stay alert to potential SPIKEs bubbling up in your organization, here's a list of ways you can predict and get in front of internal SPIKEs—some of the sharpest of all—indicated by the last two examples. Here are eight key elements of employee communications.

Communicate Major Changes in Structure, Management, or Authority

Many times internal SPIKEs or crises are caused by a lack of communication or by overcommunication. The executive staff does not provide any guidance for how the staff should talk about changes, so the staff takes it upon themselves to set the tone for the organization. This can be easily avoided with a little planning, guidance, and staff message training. To lead through change, association and corporate executives need to have crystal clear instructions about how those changes are to be communicated.

Head Off Disgruntled Employees

Organizations often have plans to deal with external crises, but nothing to deal with internal issues. To avoid a costly mistake like Goldman Sachs's, execute a well-thought-out internal communications plan when you make changes to your executive team, especially if you are a publicly traded company or an association with active members. If you leave it up to the communications gods, your constituents will wonder why the changes were made and will make up their own reasons.

Check out www.glassdoor.com, a site where former and current employees can post reviews, salaries, and benefits about an organization. It is like Yelp for recruiters, employees, and job seekers. Monitor it as soon as someone leaves, talk to other employees about how the employee felt upon dismissal, and understand potential implications or their bias. Contact an attorney to understand your rights and how you might address defamation if it becomes an issue.

Sound Out New Executives and Board Members

Leadership changes happen every year or every three years for associations. This process throws the balance off for organizations because they are trying to navigate the political waters and new board member personalities. That's why one of the first things the board and leadership should discuss is what they would do if the perfect opportunity arose for the association to comment. Start out with good scenarios and then add crisis-related scenarios. Lead a facilitated discussion and let the board discuss how they think an issue should be handled. This will provide the executive team and the staff a good guide for how they will respond when the going gets rough and have a plan of response instead of being caught off guard with a new and unprepared board. At Epic, we've done this with our clients, and they are always surprised by how board members and executives react. Do this so you're not caught off guard.

Manage Disputes between Executives and the Board

Disputes happen more often than associations and nonprofits would like to admit. One of our clients had an issue with their board trying to get involved in the association's business affairs. When the executive director decided that it was time to have a stand-alone annual meeting, the board refused to budge. Instead, they made the ED prove why this change needed to happen and argued with him to use the same scientific method the association members used in their profession. The board was concerned that the change would reflect poorly on their tenure. The board didn't want to take a chance, even though the association was losing money with the combined meeting structure. The staff at the association wasn't totally brought into the process either or messages to talk about the changes. Therefore, when the board would pull staff aside, the staff would not know what to say and that made the ED look weak.

To avoid this, executive staff needs to create internal messages when they are lobbying the board for changes. Having your employees and vendors on your side is an important part of building a case for something new, yet many leaders miss this critical part of change management.

Explain Changing Product or Service Offerings

If you make significant changes to your product or service and don't teach your employees how to communicate about it, you could find yourself with an external perception problem caused by internal miscommunication. From social media to board meetings, educating your staff is your first line of defense.

In talking with one of my nonprofit clients, she told me about one of her employees who would openly joke to donors about the fact that she didn't know where their money was going.

Be Open about Dues Increases and Pricing Changes

In my experience, many associations try to bury dues increases. One of our clients recently asked us to write a letter to members about a substantial dues increase. He did not want us to include how much the increase was going to be because they were scared of the fallout and potential loss of members. I assured him that not saying what the percentage increase would be would cause confusion and leave them vulnerable to more questions and criticism. Although this may be counterintuitive, hiding information causes a negative SPIKE. The best way to avoid this is to create a structured announcement strategy. Here are a few ways to lessen the negative impact:

- Justify the increase with what members are getting as a result of the additional dollars.
- Identify disgruntled members in advance and create a script for 5 to 8 members or staff trained to contact those select members in advance, peer to peer.
- Share a timeline for when the increases will take place.
- Offer a payment plan to show that you are flexible and understand the additional burden this is putting on members' businesses or budgets.
- Align the dues increase with survey data and information on what members want out of the organization.
- For those that you anticipate will revolt and refuse the increase and that have a history of disagreeing with the organization, create a mechanism by which they can vent their frustration and provide feedback.

Plan Messaging for Internal Conferences or Tradeshows

Many associations and nonprofits completely change the way they've always done things with little or no notice to members. Lack of knowledge causes internal gossip because employees are left to their own imaginations and messaging about how things played out. In many associations, the meetings department works in a vacuum.

ASAE has a brand strategy that other associations should mimic for its conferences. Each conference is branded, has a specific and tailored audience, and has a marketing push related to the audience's needs. It is so smart and so simple, but the approach is lost on most associations. Anyone who has ever been to the Great Ideas Conference knows that the meeting is highbrow and super creative and has a different feel from the ASAE Annual Conference. Members attending the ASAE conference have an advantage because they know what to expect, they know how to talk about the conference, and they have consistent messages that go out when people need them, based on their interest in attending the conference. Not every event will cause a SPIKE, but one could potentially happen at the meeting (good or bad) if the communications strategy isn't fully executed correctly. Planning the communications strategy isn't a SPIKE; it is basic marketing preparation.

Remember That Transparency Is Paramount

Tina Davis, executive director of communications and employee engagement at Comcast, was telling me about the efforts of the $65-billion company to create a culture of transparency. She said that the company is going through a shift in how it is run. As a result, she and her team do daily stand-up meetings. This helps her and her staff keep track of the constantly changing priorities within such a large organization. In the meeting, Davis says they discuss what they are working on and what priorities have shifted and what has emerged. "We have a highly engaged team and I keep very little secrets from my team, with very few exceptions," said Davis. She said management styles have to evolve in order to accommodate this change.

Davis told me a story about when she was leading the internal communication efforts for Merrill Lynch, during the 2008 financial crisis. She oversaw communications for more than 2,000 engineers who were writing technical code and knew very little about Wall Street. "In order to stay competitive, the technology staff had to stay focused and continue to innovate as the company dealt with the fallout of the subprime mortgage situation," Davis explained. "It fell to me and my team to keep this group of technologists in the know in order to not create panic."

She said, "We decided to do a combination of an employee survey [online], which allowed people to ask anonymous questions and hold live call-ins with executive staff. The calls began with some opening remarks that explained how the media was portraying the situation and laid out commentary from MSNBC and Fox Business. We cleared up misperceptions and explained complex financial terms and made it clear how we were moving the company forward. Additionally, we did not provide any scripts for executives, to make sure nothing seemed staged, and made the calls open to all employees. The calls were held every three to four weeks, and it was well-received."

It was important, Davis noted, "to continuously coach the executive staff on body language and word choice during that tumultuous time. We needed to show the staff that work still needed to be done and leadership had a handle on what was going on." She further explained that conversations and questions that employees asked during the call-ins gave them a sense of direction regarding the sentiment and tone to create communications that resonated based on their audience's needs.

"It all boils down to trust," Davis says. "Employees need to see, hear, and get a signal that the leaders have a grasp on the situation at hand and that issues are known, so that they have confidence in a crazy time."

Measuring the ROI of a SPIKE

"People think focus means saying yes to the thing you've got to focus on. But that's not what it means at all. It means saying no to the hundred other good ideas that there are. You have to pick carefully. I'm actually as proud of the things we haven't done as the things I have done. Innovation is saying no to 1,000 things."
—STEVE JOBS

For companies big and small, the same age-old question always comes up for marketing executives leading initiatives. How do you measure effectiveness? This question has plagued marketers for decades. Does a *New York Times* article mean more than a mention in ABC News? Is the advertising campaign actually producing results? Does social media engagement actually lead to new sales? Will the conference marketing generate enough buzz to keep us getting more members to attend year after year? You name the marketing, PR, or advertising initiative—it always comes back to how can we measure it all?

Increasingly, CMOs are forced to put specific numbers on every campaign they do. A recent study from CMO.com revealed that only 37 percent of CMOs are confident that they can provide solid numbers on initiatives they do for their organizations (*The CMO Survey* 2014). I believe this persists because CMOs are trying to measure too much, do too much, and say too much when their messages don't resonate. And they know it.

Just like Steve Jobs says, "innovation requires saying no to 1,000 other things." Same thing holds true for measuring ROI. As I mentioned in chapter 1, having a set amount of marketing and PR initiatives—SPIKEs—in one year enables you to better measure success and failure. If you are measuring a few key initiatives, three to five, you can track specifics about the campaign and do more in-depth measurement such as creating and analyzing control groups and how they respond to a marketing program, campaign, or idea. You have a beginning and end point for every SPIKE, especially in hindsight; therefore measurement is easier to prove.

If I were under oath, I would tell you the truth and nothing but the truth, which is that measuring ROI is difficult. Media interest, advertising campaigns, and a marketing initiative can yield immediate success, or they can drive actual sales months later. It may even result in nothing at all. And when results do come for any organization, many factors have to be considered, including the channel, the message, the timing, competitive differentiation … and sometimes the organization's sales team gets some credit. But, it gets easier when you *focus*.

There are countless ways people over the years have developed to measure ROI, from the Barcelona Principles to pay-per-click advertising to trying to measure consumer sentiment for a brand based on engagement. All of them fall short. The way to change this is to concentrate on specific SPIKEs. Forget trying to measure impressions, clicks, and engagement. If your initiatives don't end in generating a qualified lead or changing someone's mind, perceptions, or behavior, it didn't work. Period.

I was at a social media conference, and a speaker from a very large and well-known content marketing firm said, "Social media is the only real communications tool you can measure." I call that B.S. Engagement just shows you action, not a reaction. As a matter of fact that type of assertion is why the C-suite doesn't respect marketers or our fancy charts and made-up statistics. We are not fooling anyone, and we are opening ourselves up to the C-suite to discredit our profession because we've created measurement that is smoke and mirrors.

Katie Paine (2012), in her Measurement Blog, recommends that people define metrics that "tie their efforts to the business goals." Paine goes on to explain that "typical metrics are the percentage increase in incoming requests for information; the reduction in the amount of those who are unaware of your product offering; and the percentage of increase in the share of message penetration in designated markets or among key stakeholders."

If we isolated the SPIKEs our organization launched each year with the metric Paine recommends, we could justify the marketing spend and demonstrate real ROI.

Before we are able to implement a successful measurement program, it is up to marketers to take the executive staff aside and understand how business success is currently analyzed and use that as a baseline to create a measurement program that reflects the C-suite's goals. If we measure fewer marketing, PR, and advertising initiatives, marketers will be better able to create an argument for more budget and resources with language and explanations the C-suite can grasp. It is a scary proposition because marketers, like everyone else (and perhaps even more so), don't want to fail. It's possible that is part of the problem.

Why Failing Is Good for Marketers

What if marketers were able to fail? What if we didn't have to make up numbers such as advertising value equivalents, pay-per-click and Likes? What if we just focused on what was working and threw out ideas that bombed? Because we all know that not everything we do is pure genius. Jeff Dunsing, communications manager at ModSpace, says, "I have found many times that the marketing and sales come up with an offer that has teeth, guts and real impact. But once we screen it through the CEO, CFO, legal—they take all of the teeth out of the idea until they boil it down to something that doesn't turn heads or garner interest from our target audience."

Some of the marketing is done just to please Samantha Smith in the conference planning department because we don't want to create tension every time we see her at happy hour. I imagine you are laughing out loud as you read this because you know it is true. Now, let's talk about a method to conquer your ROI fears.

Where Do I Start?

Here are the simple rules for ROI and making a business case for your marketing and PR department. Right now businesses have all funds allocated. Therefore, getting funding for a new marketing program requires that you have to make a compelling argument for things the company can't do without. Every time we suggest an idea, we must carefully consider the opportunity cost.

Simply defined, an opportunity cost is the cost of choosing one thing over another. Executives are always weighing their options and carefully think about where they will get the most return on their investment. Understanding where and how the budget will be best used for the company or organization is the heart of budget justification and how we can really prove ROI. Choosing one program, campaign, or idea over another is the biggest hurdle CMOs face. Make it simpler. Winning ideas and campaigns that can be proven are what you want to measure—not the losers.

There are two types of financial outcomes that improve the bottom line: cost reduction (for example, a 19 percent reduction by handling customer service issues via Twitter) and increased revenue (for example, $235,000 in new customers acquired as a result of marketing). And there are nonfinancial outcomes such as new requests for information, click-through rates, new Facebook fans—the list goes on and on. The nonfinancial measurement is what most marketers focus on. According to Investopedia.com, the equation for ROI is:

$$ROI = (\text{gain from investment} - \text{cost of investment})$$
$$\div \text{ cost of investment}$$

The goal of any program is to drive conversations, create positive brand sentiment, and identify and measure conversion rates that turn into real financial impact over time. It is all about how your investment turns into gains with a series of events. How can you prove that the series of events you created is providing impact if you are cannibalizing your own marketing success with losing ideas that fall flat? That's right, you can't. That is why you need to focus on fewer, more successful, SPIKEs to prove how further investment will yield reduced costs or increased revenue. It is our job to connect the marketing and PR dots, and we can't do that effectively if the dots are scattered in a million different ideas or campaigns.

Budget for Measurement Up Front

Some people think it is costly to measure effectiveness, but the cost of not measuring is a lack of respect. Guidelines for measurement differ from industry to industry, but according to the Public

Relations Society of America (PRSA), measurement should be 5 percent of your total PR spend, including fees and pass-through costs. It may sound tedious to review where and when people are listening to you and what they are listening for, but it is an essential part of building the ROI framework. Having a good foundation enables you to build a campaign up and out with a baseline. Know why you are measuring something and what your endgame is in obtaining that information. This enables you to decrease your marketing spend while increasing your bottom-line benefits.

Get Enduring Executive Buy-In

It is essential to get everybody on board culturally and emotionally regarding the importance of measurement. Many marketers complain about getting executives to care about measurement throughout the campaign process. They start out very interested, but the interest wanes over time. I've found that even when you have buy-in, you need to have *consistent and enduring* buy-in throughout the year in order to command additional support and information from the sales force. In order to do this effectively, the focus on measurement must be a priority for senior management or there will be no accountability from the sales team. After all, what salesperson would directly attribute a big client win to a marketing initiative instead of to his or her own brilliance? When the sales team fails to tell marketing about a critical and timely issue that could lead to a SPIKE, they must be held accountable. Everyone must be held accountable for being a marketer. A lack of buy-in for marketing will affect the entire organization's bottom line. ROI is about quantifying effort and marketing spend versus revenue gained.

Always Be Closing: Getting the Sales Team on Your Side

In larger organizations, the salespeople are the eyes and ears on the ground. Many times sales and marketing don't communicate frequently enough or have the same goals. Create quarterly check-in meetings with the sales staff and report findings to senior management. If you are not getting what you need, be sure to address it immediately. There is no question, CMOs and marketers at all levels care about clicks that turn into sales leads and eventually opportunities. It has become easier than ever before to trace and track where leads come from with customer relationship management software, but that is only part of the ROI equation. According to Chet Holmes, author of *The Ultimate Sales Machine* (2007), there is a process consumers go through when buying a product or service. In the book, Holmes says buyers go through a decision-making process in the following order:

1. Do I have a problem?
2. Is there a solution for my problem?
3. Does your company/organization have a solution to that problem?
4. Do I want to buy your solution?
5. Do I need the solution *right now*?

Kristin Howard of Capital Bikeshare, a program in Washington, DC, says it is no different when she does marketing around Bike to Work Month, which occurs every May. Throughout the month of May each year, bicycle advocacy organizations flood newsfeeds on Facebook and Twitter and fill inboxes with content in an effort to promote bicycling as a transportation option. But the real opportunity to convert those who are "interested, but concerned" with biking to becoming a Capital Bikeshare members is when the month of May has passed. The next 30 to 90 days, following Bike to Work Month, is Capital Bikeshare's opportunity to SPIKE, based on the buyer pyramid/sales cone.

Create Measurable Wins

Build your campaign on what you can move the needle on. For instance, if you are the Produce Marketing Association (PMA), are you going to cure childhood obesity with your marketing initiative or are there some smaller things you can measure within a big problem? Smaller wins for PMA would include changes to school lunches, better parent education tools, and a partnership to encourage fruit and vegetable consumption state by state. Focus on bits and pieces of the issue where you can create small wins, but they must be focused on perception or behavior change that leads to more awareness. For instance, PMA recently created a partnership with Sesame Workshop to encourage families to "eat brighter!" in an effort to combat the statistic that overweight or obese children three to five years old are five times as likely to be overweight or obese as adults. The campaign gave produce companies marketing materials and the permission to use *Sesame Street* characters in packaging and in-store signage, royalty free. How did PMA track the adoption of the program? It was visible. Either the member companies used the characters in their packaging, marketing, and consumer-facing materials or they didn't.

Create a Control Group

If you are selling a product or a service related to behavior change in children, for instance, you are actually marketing to their parents. Therefore, when creating an ROI campaign consider where parents get information. Is it a parenting magazine, mommy blogs, pediatricians?

- **Qualitative research.** Set up a control group of 100 people to measure your effectiveness. Survey them after 6 months, 9 months, and 12 months to determine how behavior and perceptions may have shifted as a result of the campaign.
- **Anecdotal research.** Interview the control group participants on video in the group setting and create a compelling storyline around the changes they made.

ROI Key Takeaways

- Coordinate with your sales team.
- Coordinate with your web development team.
- Create a plan to measure and link all sales fluctuations with SPIKEs.
- Continue to pull baseline website and social media data, prior to the launch of the SPIKE, but look at this as supporting data, not as the only ROI measurement tool.
- Focus on the qualitative. How is the SPIKE being received or not being received by each of your audiences?

Where Do We Go from Here?

It has always been a dream of mine to share my experience and ignite my passion for marketing and PR in others. I hope this book has given you the tools and tenacity to pursue ideas that are right for your organization with timing as a critical element in your decision-making process. We are all drowning in a sea of content that all bleeds together, and only after a problem has been identified and a new ideal articulated can creative solutions be found.

We can no longer stand for mediocre marketing and PR—we must strive for greatness, proving that our efforts have positively affected the bottom line—anything less is unacceptable. Fight for your SPIKEs and be the executive that gets noticed. Good luck!

SPIKE Spotting: Worksheets

These worksheets are here for readers to get the most out of the SPIKE methodology. Fill out each sheet for maximum effectiveness and team-building exercises when planning, implementing, and getting your organization ready to anticipate and respond to real-time SPIKEs.

Focus on Best Success to Date

What type of marketing, PR, or social media initiative comes so naturally that it doesn't feel like work when you produce it? Brainstorm 10 and write down the ideas that you enjoyed producing, which also provided excellent ROI for your current organization or one in the past. Don't edit your answers. For now, the goal is to come up with a list of marketing wins that drew upon your strengths and brought out the *star marketer* in you.

Examples: A media pitch that resulted in an article in *Forbes* magazine; a campaign that garnered widespread engagement and interest on Facebook; an online lead-generation initiative that gave the sales team what they needed to succeed.

1. _____
   _____
   _____

2. _____
   _____
   _____

3. _____
   _____
   _____

4. _____
   _____
   _____

5. _____
   _____
   _____

6. _____

_____

_____

7. _____

_____

_____

8. _____

_____

_____

9. _____

_____

_____

10. _____

_____

_____

The goal of this exercise is to get you thinking about your past successes and realizing what worked. Identifying things that worked should help paint a better picture of what can work in the future.

Hopefully this exercise ignited some new ideas that you can begin implementing for your company, cause, or creation. If you are not sure your idea will work, get feedback from a trusted colleague or friend.

If you have gotten stumped, don't worry. We have plenty more exercises to spark ideas.

SPIKE Spotter

Go back and look at the winning marketing concepts you came up with in the past that you wrote down in the first worksheet.

Circle the ideas that you think could be adapted to provide your current organization with a unique angle and provide maximum ROI. These are potential SPIKEs where you can provide immense value to your organization.

Examples of SPIKEs:

- Trend SPIKEs. (Cupcakes. *50 Shades of Gray.* Food trucks. Warren Buffet philanthropy.)
- Pop culture/celebrity SPIKEs (Real-time Oreo and Super Bowl response. Beyoncé and Jay-Z. Kardashians.)
- Relevance SPIKEs. (Neurosurgeon—concussions in NFL. Travel industry—Air BNB. ALS Ice Bucket Challenge)
- Disaster/scandal SPIKEs. (Paula Deen's racial slur. Tiger Woods affair. Hurricane Sandy. Bridge-Gate.)
- Research SPIKEs. (Sleep deprivation related to obesity. *Harvard Business Review* article on Alzheimer's in CEOs.)
- Political SPIKEs. (Presidential campaigns. "Binders full of women." Fiscal cliff. Pundits.)
- Event SPIKEs. (Pulitzer Prize winners. Annual meeting. Academy Awards and Ellen DeGeneres.)
- Competitor SPIKEs. (T-Mobile "Break Up with Carrier" campaign. Susan G. Komen and Planned Parenthood.)

Fill out the SPIKES you are anticipating for your organization in following categories:

1. Trend SPIKEs: What trends have you seen that have or will affect your industry in the next 30, 60, 90 days?

_____

_____

_____

2. Pop culture/celebrity SPIKEs: Identify the thought-leaders and superstars of your industry, profession, or organization? How can you build on their success in your organization?

_____

_____

_____

3. Relevance SPIKEs. What's has people buzzing in your industry?

_____

_____

_____

4. Disaster/scandal SPIKEs. What previously held beliefs or misperceptions do people avoid discussing, a polarizing figure, or an issue that goes largely ignored?

_____

_____

_____

5. Research SPIKEs. What research has been released that will make people rethink previously held beliefs, ideas, or myths pertaining to your industry, profession or organization?

_____

_____

_____

6. Political SPIKEs. What legislation or political concerns/ opportunities will be affecting your industry, profession or organization in the next 30, 60, or 90 days?

_____

_____

_____

7. Event SPIKEs. What major events affect your organization, members, or customers indirectly and how will you respond to real-time SPIKE that occurs as a result of those events?

_____

_____

_____

8. Competitor SPIKEs. What have competitors said that made your customers pay attention? How can you capitalize on their success?

_____

_____

_____

Finding Your Ideal SPIKE

You're a marketer, business owner, or organizational leader, so naturally you're always thinking of ideas. Think of your ideal marketing and PR initiatives in relation to the seven principles of influence we provided in chapter 12, which include the following:

1. Authority
2. Liking
3. Commitment and consistency
4. Reciprocity
5. Scarcity
6. Social proof
7. Friendship

Use some of the SPIKE concepts you may have come up with in the last exercise. Which of the principles of influence are commonly not included in your ideas or marketing initiatives? Conversely, list every common trait these ideas have. This will help you identify new elements for ideation. Also consider factors such as timing, audience, industry focus, consumer focus, and media interest.

My ideas typically use these principles of influence:

_____

_____

_____

_____

_____

_____

I can improve my ideas by considering more concepts with these principles of influence in mind:

_____

_____

_____

_____

_____

_____

My audience would be interested in this SPIKE concept at this time because:

_____

_____

_____

_____

Describe your SPIKE so well that you can easily picture it happening to or for your organization.

_____

_____

_____

_____

The goal is to know your SPIKE so well that you can describe it to brand advocates and they can identify the signs of your SPIKEs and tell you when the change factors are coming based on detail specifics you provided.

What Does Your Current Customer Really Think?

Write everything down your current or past customers or members are experiencing with your brand—good, bad, and ugly. Be brutally honest about your organization's strengths and weaknesses.

- Write down the things your biggest fans and worst critics say about your organization.

  _____

  _____

- What do you secretly fear they know about your organization that would make them cancel their membership or refuse to purchase anything from your company?

  _____

  _____

- What organizational weaknesses do executives whisper about?

  _____

  _____

- What do you not want to talk about with valued customers or board members because it would trigger too much fear to confront?

  _____

  _____

- Write down three things your biggest competitor says about your organization to discredit what you do.

  _____

  _____

Who's Your SPIKE Audience?

1. Think of your ideal customers or members. What do they all
   have in common? List every common trait.

   Average age _____

   _____

   Income _____

   _____

   Gender _____

   _____

   Marital status _____

   _____

   Education level _____

   _____

   Industry _____

   _____

   Other professional affiliations _____

   _____

   Awards _____

   _____

   Certifications _____

   _____

   Qualifications _____

   _____

Now use those commonalities to think about *when* your audience is most likely thinking about your company, cause, or creation. Keep one potential SPIKE in mind when completing this section. Providing as much detail as you can, include a projection of needs in the near future (next 30 to 90 days), the mid-range future (6 to 12 months), and the distant future (2 years or more).

---

2. When are the big milestones in your audience's buying cycle that make them want or need to join your organization or buy your product or service?

---

3. Now that you have your audience nailed down, think about what changes would likely affect their purchasing decisions. The goal is to discern the needs of this type of person so well that you can clearly see their buying pattern.

---

4. Now that you know so much about this type of person, get inside their heads. What specific process is used to decide whether to join your organization or purchase your product or service?

_____

_____

_____

5. What will trigger them to make the purchase? The goal of this question is to understand their motivations, perceptions, and behavior so well that you can think like them, speak like them, and essentially predict when they will have a need for your product or service.

_____

_____

_____

SPIKE Plan and System

Note: This will be available online for an additional fee for people who purchase the book.

The Nine Elements of a SPIKE

ROI Plan

Communication Channels

SPIKE Brand Advocate Campaign

SPIKE Marketing and Anticipation Techniques

BONUS: SPIKE Methodology and Follow-Through Formula

Bibliography

"AAP Facts." n.d. American Academy of Pediatrics. Accessed July 6, 2014. www.aap.org/en-us/about-the-aap/aap-facts/Pages/AAP-Facts.aspx.

Associated Press. 2012. "Susan G. Komen Halts Grants to Planned Parenthood." *Politico*. February 1. www.politico.com/news/stories/0212/72289.html.

Badia, Erik, and Nancy Dillon. 2014. "Beyonce, Jay Z and Solange Knowles Pose for Happy Family Photos in New Orleans following Elevator Fight." *NY Daily News*. May 19. www.nydailynews.com/entertainment/gossip/beyonce-jay-z-solange-knowles-pose-family-photo-article-1.1798402.

Barker, Olivia. 2014. "Ellen, Brad, Julia, Meryl Snap Starriest-ever Selfie." *USA Today*. March 3. www.usatoday.com/story/life/people/2014/03/02/ellen-degeneres-oscar-selfie-a-listers/5960691/.

Barron, James. 2012. "Nation Reels After Gunman Massacres 20 Children at School in Connecticut." *New York Times*. December 14. www.nytimes.com/2012/12/15/nyregion/shooting-reported-at-connecticut-elementary-school.html?pagewanted=all&_r=0.

Belicove, Mikal E. 2011. "Measuring Offline Vs. Online Word-of-Mouth Marketing." *Entrepreneur*. November 23. www.entrepreneur.com/blog/220776.

Berger, Jonah. 2013. *Contagious: Why Things Catch On*. New York: Simon & Schuster.

Blas, Lorena, and Cindy Clark. 2013. "Experts: Paula Deen Is Done." USATODAY.COM. June 23. http://usatoday30.usatoday.com/LIFE/usaedition/2013–06–24-Paula-Deens-public-image-takes-a-hit_ST_U.htm.

Blow, Charles M. 2012. "Don't Mess With Big Bird." *New York Times*. October 5. www.nytimes.com/2012/10/06/opinion/blow-dont-mess-with-big-bird.html.

Blume, K. Allan. 2012. "'Guilty as Charged,' Cathy Says of Chick-fil-A's Stand on Biblical & Family Values." *Baptist Press.* July 16. www .bpnews.net/38271/guilty-as-charged-cathy-says-of-chickfilas-stand-on-biblical—family-values.

Bonesteel, Matt. 2014. "Jay Z, Beyonce Chat with LeBron James at Nets-Heat Game." *Washington Post.* May 13. www.washingtonpost .com/blogs/early-lead/wp/2014/05/13/jay-z-beyonce-chat-with-lebron-james-at-nets-heat-game/.

"Carnival Triumph Cruise Ship Stranded in Gulf of Mexico." 2013. WTVD-TV Raleigh-Durham. February 11. http://abc11.com/ archive/8988161/.

Carter, Brian. 2013. *The Like Economy.* Upper Saddle River, NJ: Que Publishing.

Champion, Sam, and Kate McCarthy. 2010. "Oil Spill Spreads, Napolitano Says BP Liability Waivers Unacceptable." ABC News. May 3. http://abcnews.go.com/GMA/oil-spill-spreads-gulf-bp-calls-liability-waivers/story?id=10536850.

"Chick-fil-A Exec Takes Stance against Same-sex Marriage." 2012. USATODAY.COM. July 9. http://usatoday30.usatoday.com/ money/companies/story/2012–07–19/Chik-fil-A-gay-marriage/ 56336116/1.

Chumley, Cheryl K. 2013. "Lululemon Athletica Chairman Quits after Firestorm over His Fat-thighs Comment." *Washington Times.* December 10. www.washingtontimes.com/news/2013/dec/10/ lululemon-athletic-wear-chair-quits-over-firestorm/.

Cialdini, Robert B. 2007. *Influence: The Psychology of Persuasion.* New York: Collins.

The CMO Survey. August 2014. http://cmosurvey.org/files/2014/09/ The_CMO_Survey-Highlights_and_Insights-Aug-2014.pdf.

CNN Political Unit. 2012. "Transcript of Wednesday's Presidential Debate." CNN.com. October 4. www.cnn.com/2012/10/03/ politics/debate-transcript/index.html.

Coca-Cola. 2014. "Coca-Cola | House Rules." Facebook. July 2. https:// www.facebook.com/cocacola/app_153692631322774.

Colgrass, Neal. 2013. "2.7M Updated Facebook Pic for Gay Marriage." Newser. March 30. www.newser.com/story/165374/millions-update-facebook-pic-for-gay-marriage.html.

Condon, Stephanie. 2012. "Planned Parenthood Raises $3M for Breast Care Services in Wake of Susan G. Komen Flap." CBSNews. February 3. www.cbsnews.com/news/planned-parenthood-raises-3m-for-breast-care-services-in-wake-of-susan-g-komen-flap/.

Davis, Allison P. 2014. "Beyoncé Posted 4 Happy Solange Pictures on Instagram." The Cut. nymag.com. May 14. http://nymag.com/thecut/2014/05/beyonc-posted-4-solange-pictures-on-instagram.html.

Deggans, Eric. 2013. "Lauer's Interview with Paula Deen Missed the Real Questions." Poynter. June 27. www.poynter.org/latest-news/top-stories/216994/lauers-interview-with-paula-deen-missed-the-real-questions/.

Douglas, Tyler. 2014. "4 Reasons Why CMO Tenure Will Continue to Increase." CMO.com. April 24. www.cmo.com/articles/2014/4/16/_4_reasons_why_cmo_t.html.

Durando, Jessica. 2010. "BP's Tony Hayward: 'I'd Like My Life Back.'" USA Today. June 1. http://content.usatoday.com/communities/greenhouse/post/2010/06/bp-tony-hayward-apology/1#.UMYlISKCWSo.

Eisingerich, Andreas B., HaeEun Chun, Yeyi Liu, Jia He, and Simon J. Bell. 2014. "Why Recommend a Brand Face-to-face but Not on Facebook? How Word-of-mouth on Online Social Sites Differs from Traditional Word-of-mouth." Journal of Consumer Psychology, May 29. DOI: 10.1016/j.jcps.2014.05.004.

Epic PR Group Staff. 2012a. "Kony 2012 and the 'Bounce Effect.'" The Public Relations Heat Index. March 9. http://prheatindex.epicprgroup.com/2012/03/kony-2012-and-the-bounce-effect/.

Epic PR Group Staff. 2012b. "Preventing Crisis: Tip #12—The Art of the Apology." The Public Relations Heat Index. April 26. http://prheatindex.epicprgroup.com/2012/04/preventing-crisis-tip-12-the-art-of-the-apology/.

Epic PR Group Staff. 2013. "The Psychology of Believing: Cognitive Effects That Influence Communications." The Public Relations Heat Index. February 13. http://prheatindex.epicprgroup.com/2012/02/the-psychology-of-believing-cognitive-affects-that-influence-communications/.

ET Online Staff. 2013. "Lance Admits: Winning's Impossible without Doping." ET Online. January 17. www.etonline.com/news/129345_Lance_Armstrong_Confesses_to_Doping_During_All_Seven_Tour_De_France_Wins/index.html.

Evangelista, Benny. 2009. "How Domino's Responded to Prank Video." SFGate. May 3. www.sfgate.com/business/article/How-Domino-s-responded-to-prank-video-3163363.php.

Fekadu, Mesfin. 2014. "Beyonce, Jay Z, Solange Moving past Attack Video." The Associated Press. May 15. http://bigstory.ap.org/article/beyonce-jay-z-solange-moving-past-attack-video.

France, Lisa Respers, and Marc Balinsky. 2014. "Did Beyonce's Sister Fight Jay Z?" CNN. May 12. www.cnn.com/2014/05/12/showbiz/celebrity-news-gossip/jay-z-solange-beyonce/index.html

Galant, Gregory. 2012. "Why Public Relations Gets No Respect." *Fortune.* November 15. http://fortune.com/2012/11/15/why-public-relations-gets-no-respect/.

Gesenhues, Amy. 2014. "Arby's Social Media Manager Gives Inside Scoop on Tweet to Pharrell That Rocked the Grammys." Marketing Land. January 29. http://marketingland.com/guy-behind-arbys-tweet-pharrell-williams-rocked-grammys-72222.

Godin, Seth. 2008. *Tribes: We Need You to Lead Us.* New York: Portfolio.

Greengard, Samuel. 2013. "Dealing With Distraction." CMO.com. July 22. www.cmo.com/articles/2013/7/15/dealing_with_distrac.html.

Grohol, John M. 2011. "FOMO Addiction: The Fear of Missing Out." Psych Central.com. April 14. http://psychcentral.com/blog/archives/2011/04/14/fomo-addiction-the-fear-of-missing-out/.

Hardy, Rebecca. 2009. "'I'm Quite Odd. I Do Get Very Dark Moods': Simon Cowell's Most Revealing—and Surprising—Interview Ever." Mail Online. May 22. www.dailymail.co.uk/tvshowbiz/article-1185451/Im-quite-odd-I-dark-moods-Simon-Cowells-revealing—surprising—interview-ever.html.

Hari, Vani. 2014a. "Subway: Stop Using Dangerous Chemicals In Your Bread." Food Babe. February 4. http://foodbabe.com/subway/.

Hari, Vani. 2014b. "The One Thing Subway Is Still Hiding from All of Us!" Food Babe. February 7. http://foodbabe.com/2014/02/07/subway-update/.

Hensley, Scott. 2012. "Planned Parenthood Controversy Hangs over Komen's Fundraising Races." NPR. June 1. www.npr.org/blogs/health/2012/06/01/154135526/planned-parenthood-controversy-hangs-over-komens-fundraising-races.

Holmes, Chet. 2007. *The Ultimate Sales Machine.* New York: Portfolio.

Horn, Sam. 2006. *POP: Create the Perfect Pitch, Title, and Tagline for Anything.* New York: Perigree.

Hornbuckle, David. 2009. "The Oprah Effect." Inc.com. August 4. www.inc.com/articles/2009/08/oprah.html.

Horton, Mark. 2011. "#E2sday: The Hectic Schedule of a Social Media Manager." Socialcast. February 15. http://blog.socialcast.com/e2sday-the-hectic-schedule-of-a-social-media-manager/.

"Interview for Press Association (10th Anniversary as Prime Minister)." 1989. Interview by Chris Moncrieff. Margaret Thatcher Foundation. May 3. www.margaretthatcher.org/document/107427.

Invisible Children. 2012. *KONY 2012.* YouTube. March 5. https://www
.youtube.com/watch?v=Y4MnpzG5Sqc.

Jenkins, Sally. 2012. "Lance Armstrong Doping Campaign Exposes
USADA's Hypocrisy." *Washington Post.* August 24. www.washington
post.com/sports/othersports/lance-armstrong-doping-campaign-
exposes-usadas-hypocrisy/2012/08/24/858a13ca-ee22-11e1-afd6-
f55f84bc0c41_story.html

"Lance Edward Armstrong." n.d. Bio.com. Accessed July 16, 2014.
www.biography.com/people/lance-armstrong-9188901.

Lauckner, Sally. 2014. "ALS Ice Bucket Challenge Has Nonprofits
Rethinking 'Public Relations Dollars.'" *Huffington Post.* August 22.
www.huffingtonpost.com/2014/08/22/ice-bucket-challenge-
success_n_5701218.html.

Lee, Kevan. 2014. "The Social Media Frequency Guide: How Often
to Post to Facebook, Twitter, LinkedIn, and More." Fast Com-
pany.com. April 15. www.fastcompany.com/3029019/work-smart/
the-social-media-frequency-guide-how-often-to-post-to-facebook-
twitter-linkedin-a.

Leibowitz, Brandon. 2012. "Optimum Facebook Posting Times." Social
Media Today. October 9. www.socialmediatoday.com/content/
optimum-facebook-posting-times.

Levien, Simone. 2014. "Forrester." B2B Marketers Struggle to Connect
Content Marketing With Business Value. July 16. www.forrester
.com/B2B%2BMarketers%2BStruggle%2BTo%2BConnect%
2BContent%2BMarketing%2BWith%2BBusiness%2BValue/-/
E-PRE7144.

Luo, Xueming, Michael Wiles, and Sascha Raithel. 2013. "Making the
Most of a Polarizing Brand." *Harvard Business Review.* November.
http://hbr.org/2013/11/make-the-most-of-a-polarizing-brand/
ar/1.

McInerny, Thomas K. 2012. "Statement in Response to the Elementary
School Shooting in Connecticut." American Academy of Pediatrics. December 14. www.aap.org/en-us/about-the-aap/aap-press-
room/Pages/Statement-in-Response-to-the-Elementary-School-
Shooting-in-Connecticut.aspx.

Monga, Aloparna Basu, and Deborah Roedder John. 2007. "Cultural
Differences in Brand Extension Evaluation: The Influence of
Analytic versus Holistic Thinking." *Journal of Consumer Research* 33
(March): 529–536. www.researchgate.net/publication/23547353_
Cultural_Differences_in_Brand_Extension_Evaluation_The_
Influence_of_Analytic_versus_Holistic_Thinking/file/72e7e52bb
535a8f50d.pdf.

Moskin, Julia. 2012. "Chef Has Diabetes, and Some Say 'I Told You So.'" *New York Times*. January 17. www.nytimes.com/2012/01/18/dining/paula-deen-says-she-has-type-2-diabetes.html?pagewanted=all&_r=0.

Mungin, Lateef, and Mark Morgenstein. 2013. "Carnival Cruise Line in More Troubled Waters." CNN. March 16. www.cnn.com/2013/03/15/travel/carnival-problems/.

Neff, Jack. 2012. "Marketers Are Getting Worse at Directing Their Budgets Wisely." *Advertising Age*. May 28. http://adage.com/article/news/marketers-worse-directing-budgets-wisely/235009/.

Nelson, Jared. 2014. "Rovio Announces a Soft-Launch for a New 'Angry Birds' Game." Touch Arcade. March 10. http://toucharcade.com/2014/03/10/new-angry-birds-teaser-2/.

Paharia, Neeru, Anat Keinan, Jill Avery, and Juliet B. Schor. 2011. "The Underdog Effect: The Marketing of Disadvantage and Determination through Brand Biography." *Journal of Consumer Research* 37(5): 775–790. http://EconPapers.repec.org/RePEc:ucp:jconrs:doi:10.1086/656219.

Paine, Katie. 2012. "The Conclave's Social Media Measurement Standards 2013." http://painepublishing.com/social-media-measurement-standards-2013/

Parmar, Neil. 2013. "How Blake Mycoskie Got His Groove Back." *Entrepreneur*. September 26. http://m.entrepreneur.com/article/228578.

PBS. 2012. "PBS Statement Regarding October 3 Presidential Debate." News release. October 4. PBS. www.pbs.org/about/news/archive/2012/statement-presidential-debate/.

"Pediatricians Can Offer Care for Grieving Families after the Loss of a Child." 2012. American Academy of Pediatrics. November 26. www.aap.org/en-us/about-the-aap/aap-press-room/pages/Pediatricians-Can-Offer-Care-For-Grieving-Families-After-the-Loss-of-a-Child.aspx.

Planned Parenthood. 2012. "'Alarmed and Saddened' by Komen Foundation Succumbing to Political Pressure, Planned Parenthood Launches Fund for Breast Cancer Services." News release. Planned Parenthood. January 31. www.plannedparenthood.org/planned-parenthood-southwest-central-florida/newsroom/press-releases/alarmed-saddened-komen-foundation-succumbing-political-pressure-planned-parenthood-launches-fun.

"Power Women." 2014. *Forbes*. September 17. www.forbes.com/profile/sara-blakely/.

PR Epicenter. 2012. "Preparing For a Crisis: Trust Trumps Likeability." CommPRObiz.com. December 27. www.commpro.biz/pr-epicenter/preparing-crisis-trust-trumps-likeability/.

Ramisetti, Kirthana. 2014. "Jay Z, Solange Knowles Elevator Fight Mocked on 'SNL,' Maya Rudolph Makes Surprise Appearance as Beyonce." *NY Daily News.* May 18. www.nydailynews.com/entertainment/tv/jay-z-solange-elevator-fight-mocked-snl-article-1.1796878.

"Remarks from the NRA Press Conference on Sandy Hook School Shooting, Delivered on Dec. 21, 2012 (Transcript)." 2012. *Washington Post.* December 21. www.washingtonpost.com/politics/remarks-from-the-nra-press-conference-on-sandy-hook-school-shooting-delivered-on-dec-21–2012-transcript/2012/12/21/bd1841fe-4b88–11e2-a6a6-aabac85e8036_story.html.

Rishe, Patrick. 2013. "Doping Confession to Help Livestrong Foundation More Than Lance Armstrong's Future Personal Earnings." *Forbes.* January 14. www.forbes.com/sites/prishe/2013/01/14/doping-confession-to-help-livestrong-foundation-more-than-lance-armstrongs-future-personal-earnings/.

Rubin, Ben Fox, and Andrew Dowell. 2013. "Lululemon Offers Weak Sales Outlook." *Wall Street Journal.* December 12. http://online.wsj.com/news/articles/SB10001424052702303293604579253882031794794.

Schwartz, Nelson D. 2012. "Public Exit From Goldman Raises Doubt over a New Ethic." *New York Times.* March 14. www.nytimes.com/2012/03/15/business/a-public-exit-from-goldman-sachs-hits-a-wounded-wall-street.html.

Scott, David Meerman. 2012. *Real-Time Marketing and PR.* Hoboken, NJ: Wiley.

Sernovitz, Andy. 2012. *Word of Mouth Marketing.* Austin, TX: Greenleaf.

Shaw, Alexis. "12 Companies That Have Cut Ties with Paula Deen." 2013. ABC News. June 29. http://abcnews.go.com/Business/paula-deens-empire-continues-crumble-wake-racial-slurs/story?id=19534224.

Smith, Greg. 2012. "Why I Am Leaving Goldman Sachs." *New York Times.* March 13. www.nytimes.com/2012/03/14/opinion/why-i-am-leaving-goldman-sachs.html?_r=1.

Stafford, Leon. 2014. "Cathy Seeks to Put Gay Marriage Flap behind Chick-fil-A." *Atlanta Journal Constitution.* March 14. www.myajc.com/news/business/cathy-seeks-to-put-gay-marriage-flap-behind-chick-/nfCHj/.

Stanley, T. L. 2010. "Russell Weiner, Domino's." *AdWeek*. September 13. www.adweek.com/news/2010/russell-weiner-dominos-94411.

Strachan, Maxwell. 2013. "Lululemon Founder 'Really Sad' He Offended Women." *Huffington Post*. November 11. www.huffington post.com/2013/11/11/lululemon-apology-womens-bodies_n_ 4254594.html.

Strait, Michelle. 2014. "Soft Launch vs. Hard Launch." Small Business. http://smallbusiness.chron.com/soft-launch-vs-hard-launch- 24486.html.

Strange, Adario. 2013. "Garage Where Steve Jobs Started Apple Designated as Historic Site." Mashable. October 29. http://mashable .com/2013/10/29/steve-jobs-apple-garage-landmark/.

Strom, Stephanie. 2014. "CVS Vows to Quit Selling Tobacco Products." *New York Times*. February 5. www.nytimes.com/2014/02/06/ business/cvs-plans-to-end-sales-of-tobacco-products-by-october .html.

Sullivan, Sean. 2012. "NRA's Wayne LaPierre: Put 'Armed Police Officers' in Every School." *Washington Post*. December 21. www.washingtonpost.com/blogs/post-politics/wp/2012/12/21/ nras-wayne-lapierre-put-armed-police-officers-in-every-school/.

Susan G. Komen. 2012. "Statement from Susan G. Komen Board of Directors and Founder and CEO Nancy G. Brinker." News release. Susan G. Komen. February 3. http://ww5.komen.org/ KomenNewsArticle.aspx?id=19327354148.

Swift, Art. 2014. "Americans Say Social Media Have Little Sway on Purchases." Gallup Economy. June 24. www.gallup.com/poll/171785/ americans-say-social-media-little-effect-buying-decisions.aspx?utm_ source=alert&utm_medium=email&utm_campaign=syndication&& utm_content=morelink&utm_term=All%20Gallup%20Headlines.

TD Bank. 2014. "Sometimes You Just Want to Say Thank You #TDThanksYou." YouTube. July 24. https://www.youtube.com/ watch?v=bUkN7g_bEAI.

"Thomas K. McInerny, MD, FAAP." n.d. Accessed July 2, 2014. www.aap .org/en-us/about-the-aap/aap-press-room/aap-press-room-media- center/Pages/Thomas-K-McInerny-Bio.aspx.

Thomson, Katherine. 2009. "Simon Cowell: I'm Quite Odd, I Have Dark Moods." *Huffington Post*. May 24. www.huffingtonpost.com/ 2009/05/24/simon-cowell-im-quite-odd_n_207140.html.

Tilley, Jonathan. 2014. "Inside Malaysia Airlines' Crisis Response to the Plane Disappearance." *PRWeek*. March 24. www.prweek.com/ article/1286521/inside-malaysia-airlines-crisis-response-plane- disappearance.

US Department of Education. 2011. National Center for Education Statistics. *Academic Libraries: 2010.* Ed. Tai Phan, Laura Hardesty, Jamie Hug, and Cindy Sheckells. December. http://nces.ed.gov/pubs2012/2012365.pdf.

Vaynerchuk, Gary. 2013. *Jab, Jab, Jab, Right Hook: How to Tell Your Story in a Noisy Social World.* New York: HarperCollins.

Wanucha, M., and L. Hofschire. 2013. *U.S. Public Libraries and the Use of Web Technologies, 2012 (Closer Look Report).* Denver, CO: Colorado State Library, Library Research Service.

Wasserman, Todd. 2011. "Domino's Pizza Runs Unfiltered Customer Comments on Times Square Billboard." Mashable. July 25. http://mashable.com/2011/07/25/dominos-comments-times-square/.

Weiner, Rachel. 2013. "Mark Sanford Wins South Carolina Special Election." *Washington Post.* May 7. www.washingtonpost.com/blogs/post-politics/wp/2013/05/07/mark-sanford-wins-south-carolina-special-election/.

Whitler, Kimberly A. 2013. "Are CMOs Unfit for the Job? How the CEO Can Make a Difference." *Chief Executive.* July 10. http://chiefexecutive.net/are-cmos-unfit-for-the-job-how-the-ceo-can-make-a-difference.

Wolfgang, Ben. 2014. "Obama Takes Aim at 'Corporate Deserters,'" *Washington Times.* July 24. www.washingtontimes.com/news/2014/jul/24/obama-takes-aim-corporate-deserters/#ixzz38lv00ImR Arantxa.

York, Emily Bryson. 2009. "Domino's Posts Apology Video on YouTube." *Advertising Age.* April 15. http://adage.com/article/news/domino-s-youtube-nightmare-continues/136015/.

Index